Connecting with Horses

The Life Lessons We Can Learn from Horses

Margrit Coates

Ulysses Press

Published in the U.S. by
ULYSSES PRESS
P.O. Box 3440
Berkeley, CA 94703
www.ulyssespress.com

First published in the U.K. in 2008 by Rider, an imprint of Ebury Publishing

ISBN10: 1-56975-691-0
ISBN13: 978-1-56975-691-1
Library of Congress Catalog Number: 2008906995

Cover design: Two Associates
Cover photography: Sabine Stuewer
U.S. Editor: Jennifer Privateer
Editorial Associates: Elyce Petker, Lauren Harrison
Production: Tamara Kowalski

Printed in Canada by Webcom

10 9 8 7 6 5 4 3 2 1

Distributed by Publishers Group West

PLEASE NOTE:

The information given in this book is not intended to be taken as a replacement or substitute for professional veterinary or medical advice. A veterinarian must always be consulted for any problem or concerns whatsoever with an equine. Neither the author nor the publisher can be held responsible for any loss or claim arising out of the use or misuse of the suggestions made in this book, nor the failure to take and adhere to professional veterinary or medical advice.

I dedicate this book to the memory of Uschi, my late mother,
who helps and guides me from heaven.

Life has many ups and downs and twists and turns, but you are going to spend some healing time with a very special teacher, someone highly recommended and very accomplished. When you meet, your senses are submerged, your heart recognizes someone you know from a long time ago in your evolution. The wise eyes hold your attention, seeing you within and without, the presence is unique and listens attentively in a way that no one else has ever done before. You bare your soul and by acute observations of your thoughts and emotions, the teacher reflects back to you things that you had not previously been aware of. There is nothing covert or judgmental in the approach, only a benign desire to help. Without using words, the teacher can change your life. You reach out and touch the loving face, feel the warm breath on your hands, stroke the soft body. You are saved. This guide is your horse, and all horses in the world.

Contents

Foreword

Margrit Coates has a lot of nerve. And grace. It's a disarming combination. Her influential books, *Healing for Horses* and *Horses Talking*, dared to challenge conventional notions of equine intelligence, acknowledging these quite obviously powerful creatures as spiritual beings back when the average horse "owner" was disinclined to admit they were sentient, let alone capable of teaching their human caretakers a thing or two.

Making serious inroads as an animal communicator before the notion was widely tolerated, let alone accepted, Margrit herself was not immune to the controversy her first book might create. Nearing publication, she seriously considered buying up all available copies before they hit the stores. Thankfully, vision won out, and she was rewarded with the support of many people who secretly *felt* what she had the courage to declare publicly, and hence irrevocably, in writing.

Twenty-first-century science is finally catching up to what seemed like witchcraft or wishful thinking a mere decade ago, and Margrit Coates is riding the crest of a wave. *Connecting with Horses* shows compassionately, intelligently, and critically the many ways that horses help humans, teaching life lessons relevant beyond the barn, both informally to riders, and formally as co-facilitators in the fast-growing fields of equine-facilitated therapy, experiential education, leadership coaching, and consciousness research. While exploring the ramifications of this most recent development, she delves more deeply than some innovators in these fields are willing to go, questioning the appropriateness of emerging practices while recognizing their potential to reinvigorate the very heart and soul of humanity.

The author's balance of research, anecdotes, and expertise communicates years of careful questioning and innovation drawn from personal transformation. She not only listens to horses, she allows them to move her to the core. And she encourages us to do the same, foreshadowing a time when the human race will finally let the "horse nation" claim its rightful status as a conscious partner in our own species' evolution.

Our ancestors mapped the world on horseback. As waves of

explorers, crusaders, and conquistadors surged across the continents, both species benefited *and* suffered as a result of the proverbial pioneering spirit. Yet when we finally acknowledge that we're riding a race of intelligent, soulful beings, the journey doesn't end. A strange new world materializes, seemingly out of nowhere, and we realize these proud, strong, brave yet sensitive beings are urging us onward.

Margrit Coates is a worthy translator of this multifaceted, downright multidimensional, equine lesson plan: the vast and unpredictable adventure of mapping consciousness itself. I, for one, am honored and inspired to be one of the first to read this important book, and I recommend it wholeheartedly to others.

Linda Kohanov

Author of *The Tao of Equus,*
Riding between the Worlds, and
Way of the Horse: Equine Archetypes for Self Discovery
September, 2007
Sonoita, Arizona

Introduction

I have long since given up thinking that there would come a point when my knowledge gained through horses would become stagnant, or that I would need to follow another realm of exploration to further my understanding of self and the universe. What we can learn about the horse is a never-ending journey, and even though I have been involved with many thousands of them I have not met one identical to another. Every horse is a teacher and a healer, and what is offered becomes geared to what we need at the time. The horse is many things, and has become my greatest teacher. Certainly, since I stepped into the arena of delving deeply into horses, it has felt like a continuous lesson.

Horses have brought people and opportunities into my life that I could not have imagined occurring. Through my work with horses, I have visited the U.S. several times, including being invited to the stunningly beautiful Rocking C's ranch in Montana to attend a unique Horseman's week. Meeting famous horsemen and horsewomen from both the U.S. and Europe, all promoting the welfare of horses on a deep level, was inspirational. It was there that I met the amazing Phillip Whiteman, Jr. and his paint pony Sioux Boy. Phillip is a Northern Cheyenne Indian and has similar views to me about horses belonging to the horse nation, being our mirror, and that all life is connected. One evening I joined the other ranch guests gathered by the spectacular Smith River to listen to Phillip's story telling. As Phillip talked about rainbow colors in his traditional clothing, a real rainbow appeared in the sky behind where he stood, arcing majestically over the silvery colored river. Then Phillip talked about eagle feathers in his headdress, and suddenly a bald eagle flew slowly along the river towards the rainbow, before circling around us. It was awesome to watch. There was more to come however . . . one of Phillip's stories involved a duck, and a mother duck suddenly came paddling down the river followed by a brood of ducklings! We were all stunned and the whole event was incredibly spiritual. I felt so honored that my work with horses had led me to that unique and life-enhancing experience. When we spiritually connect to horses, magical things can indeed happen.

Writing now about how horses help and heal us completes a trilogy of learning. My first book, *Healing for Horses*, is about how we can be healers of horses; the second, *Horses Talking*, explains how to communicate with them; and this third book brings together the foundation of what it is all about. Without the support of the horse, life would lose direction and be empty for a great many people.

As time passed in writing this book I needed to come up with a title, and I knew that ultimately I would be helped in this matter by horses. My mentor eventually appeared in the shape of a horse called Ollie. Ollie belongs to a friend called Alison, and while talking to her I knew that the horse would be taking it all in, as they always do. I was hoping for some insight and sure enough ideas started to form in my mind about the horse as a unique teacher and a powerful healer. Through communicating with Ollie I was given confirmation about the content that horses collectively wanted me to include, but what should I call the book itself?

After pausing for a couple of minutes, Alison said, "Ollie has just told me that the title for your new book has been covered in our conversation." As we had been talking for over an hour, we had dealt with a lot of topics so that clue was rather vague, I felt. We started to recap our discussion about learning from horses and connecting with them.

Ollie snorted very loudly in my face and at last I paid full attention. After mulling some ideas over for a few minutes, I thanked the horse for his message and told him that the book would be called *Connecting with Horses*. He looked very pleased with his pupil. Although horses give us clues, the thinking and the decision-making ultimately have to be ours.

Putting this book together has taken me on an amazing journey, a learning and discovery in itself. As I investigated and explored the many areas in which horses help and heal people, as well as gathering information from clients and acquaintances, my own awareness expanded. Each encounter with either a horse or a person helped further unlock my inner resources and enhanced my healing communication gifts. It seems that there is no end to what the horse is capable of activating.

The irrefutable evidence is there. The horse tunes into us on a very deep level. Horses specifically teach me that they have a desire to help nature and humankind reconcile. Through horse care and understanding, we can learn self-care and people care. Yet there is far more— through associating with horses I have learned how to gain insight into the grand scheme of things.

Horses symbolize soul and life energy, and it is that which connects most powerfully to me. Swiss psychologist Carl Jung (1875–1961) talked about the collective unconscious, which he said was common to all people and animals. Jung also theorized about psychological discord resulting from a disconnection with a person's life energy. For myself, and for others the world over, connection of personal life energy to the collective unconscious comes through a reciprocal love affair with horses.

Horses can lift from us the binding ties of myths and misunderstandings, so that we become united with the horse in a place where ignorance is replaced with wisdom. The Centaur is depicted as a half-human, half-horse creature, representing the symbolic connection between the two, and resulting in a blending of both spirits. Through connecting with the horse we not only blend, but we are healed at our core. Horses wish to share their unique gifts with us, and offer them continuously. My purpose throughout this book is to share what horses have taught me, and in doing so to invoke images and thoughts that your own heart and soul remembers regarding horses, and to help you understand them on a deep level.

Just before I wrote the last chapter I spent some time with a herd of thoroughbred horses on the Sussex Downs. It was a gloriously sunny day and with horses around me, birdsong and distant views of the sea, it felt like heaven. I let the everyday drift away, and absorbed the world and the spirit of the horse. As I became still within, I asked one particular horse that I was drawn to, "Tell me, what is the special lesson that I need to learn today?"

My heart felt light, as the wise horse spoke to my soul: "Know who you are and be who you are."

The horse then paused, before adding, "We are the spirit of love . . . that is at the heart of each lesson that we offer."

Margaret Coates

1 What's so special about horses?

Connecting with horses is letting go, yet merging, to enter the infinite and dance with the spirit of the horse, a magical moment of mutual respect, harmony, and partnership. Through this union, anything and everything is possible and we can become whatever we give ourselves the power to be. Sometimes the connection happens without effort; at other times it's something that we yearn for, seemingly elusive and tentative.

She had seen me from about a quarter of a mile away. I don't know what she had been doing until then, because it was a while before I noticed her properly and then it took longer to realize that she was heading straight towards me and not just wandering aimlessly. It was an eerie wait as she strode purposefully forward, head held high, as though she had been waiting for me to arrive at that exact moment. For a second, irrationally, I thought she was going to bowl me over, she came at me with such energy, but then why would she want to do that? She stopped right in front of me, almost touching me, but not quite, her face directly in front of mine, so that I swayed back onto my heels. I was not afraid, sensing that this female did not wish me harm, even though she stared at me with such intensity that I felt the hairs stand up on the back of my neck.

My heart started to race and I wondered what was coming, as the gaze held me motionless, expectant. An age seemed to pass by, but it can only have been a minute or so, and I was intrigued by her intention. What did she want, I wondered, and asking, received no reply.

For someone whose specialty is interspecies communication it felt like I had entered a classroom having forgotten my books, paper, pen. I felt strangely powerless, yet spellbound. I caught sight of her friends going about their business, aware but not bothered that I was not of their kin. Suddenly the spell was broken and my heartbeat slowed to normal again, which gave me the confidence to want to reach out and make contact, to see if that gave me a clue about why she had singled me out. Raising my hand, I lightly touched her forehead, and was inspired to do so as a blessing. She sighed, then, turning her head, my new friend looked toward her kind before moving in that direction.

I sat down on a mound nearby and for the next half an hour or so she stayed close, watchfully grazing. Had this free-roaming brown horse been a pet at one time, used to human company; maybe that was the reason for her interest? Just as I was about to leave, she came over to again stand directly before me. This time I asked her what it was that I should know? Her eyes absorbed me, washed over me, and looked through me. There were no words and I realized that I didn't require bits of paper to write my lessons on because she was inscribing them onto my heart, turning a page in the book that is my soul and adding a paragraph or two of wisdom. I knew that her teaching was an infusion of pure knowledge and that some time, when I needed it, I would reap the benefit.

The horse made such an impression on me that I wanted, needed, to see her again and so I returned the next day, but the herd had moved on, leaving me with a sense of profound loss. Wandering around, I eventually found it again and when the mare saw me, she came over in the same manner as before. It was like a clandestine meeting of lovers as we walked together for a while out onto the open plain.

Once more I went back to find her, but then lost contact; the New Forest National Park is a big place where many herds roam. Several times a week when crossing the park I look out for her, wondering where she is, hoping she is safe and whether she now has a foal by her side teaching it all that she knows. Our time together was fleeting, but that connection is permanent, meaning far more to me than to her, although perhaps not. Maybe I do horses an injustice by thinking that they don't really need us. What I do know is that out there, somewhere, a spiritual master exists, her

kind producing many around the world. The glimpse of the mare's presence that day took my breath away in just the same way that what horses reveal often does. As with many experiences in life, I came upon the event unexpectedly, and something irrevocably shifted. I miss her, but she lives within my essence and sometimes you do not need to know what you have learned, just that you have. Our meeting was a lesson in, and of, itself.

The way of the horse

Horse: the very word invokes many things—a large, beautiful, and majestic animal and the archetype of power, freedom, gracefulness, and wild energy. The horse also stirs passions with a tremendous capacity to reach our hearts, stimulating ability to nurture and love, as well as demonstrating affection back. There is a rich and complex symbolism attached to the horse, which links us back in both time and consciousness. In Celtic mythology, the horse represents fertility and in Native American culture, the horse's revered attributes include love, devotion, and physical/spiritual power. Shamans are often depicted flying on mythical horses. Once experienced in some way the horse becomes enmeshed in our future, and already forms part of our history, having a unique relationship with humanity. Through our historical connection with horses, we are encoded to be involved with them, as throughout the ages they have played a key role in civilization, which can be traced across most cultures. Horses have been revered and cherished, or abused and misunderstood—processes continuing to this day. Nowadays, almost entirely domesticated, although the horse itself does not know that, inherent instincts remain exactly the same as those of the wild horse, whatever the age or gender. Adapting a great deal to live alongside and partner with humans, the domesticated horse has sacrificed social hierarchy with its own kind and a free, roaming lifestyle.

However, even though in the West horses are not now needed for our physical survival, interest in being with them is escalating. At a subliminal level, humankind intrinsically has an inkling that horses can assist with our spiritual survival and seeds of spiritual vitality become sown in us through knowing them. Even though they may no longer work for us, horses work on and with us, which is why, increasingly, contact with horses is recommended for therapeutic reasons. Horses can have an immeasurable restorative effect on human beings, as our interaction with them triggers an awakening of long-forgotten abilities as well as the emergence of attributes we didn't know existed within us.

> **"** Stepping up to a horse is the beginning of an adventure whereby we stand poised on the brink of personal discovery. **"**

The way of the horse is to speak to hearts, minds, and souls, helping improve perception, not only of ourselves but of others, and inspiring us to overcome the imbalances of life. There are many awesome facets to horses and their very proximity can help people who are troubled, sick, disadvantaged, or otherwise seeking revelation, and who wish to achieve a sense of improved well-being. It seems that even watching images of a horse can trigger a deep emotional response in people. In their book *Horse Sense and the Human Heart,* Adele von Rüst McCormick and Marlena Deborah McCormick write about how they made films of horses, which were shown to people who were confined in some way and unable to get outside. Many of those who watched the films described an enrichment of their lives, including a dimension of peace. Not surprisingly, these people also expressed a desire to see the horses in person so that all their senses could be fully stimulated.

The tamed wildness of the horse is our link to untamed wildness stirring within us, hidden memories of human awareness going back in time—a very powerful energy footprint for us to connect with. The horse is our highway to nature and the source of the natural world, a connector for unity with the universe.

In his book *How to Be Wild*, Simon Barnes explains that without an element of the non-human in our lives, we are not properly human. He says, "I have wildness all around me when I am at home: most of it is in the hearts and minds of my horses." About working with a young horse, Barnes continues, "I sought not to lose the wildness but to canalize; to explore the extraordinary affinity between our two species, and to establish that intoxicating cooperation, that sense of two wills working as one."

Through being with horses we are offered clues to answer the question that we frequently ask ourselves: "Who am I and what's life all about?" We are helped by rekindling a memory of who we are, and in doing so we are reminded to appreciate them for who *they* are. The horse doesn't actually "do" anything to us in a physical sense, but somehow has an amazing ability to help us get in touch with our self-regulatory system through which a reversion to inner harmony can take place. The horse points the way and we make the journey.

> **"**To see and touch a horse stirs archetypal energies arising from primitive images present in the collective consciousness.**"**

Discovery

When a horse touches our lives, we can learn on many levels as he or she becomes our teacher, guide, and supporter. The experience can be so cathartic that life is never the same again. Even for those of us who spend a lot of time in the presence of horses it's a continuing evolutionary process. That is if we want it to be so, for ultimately the choice is ours to accept or decline what is offered. Time spent with a horse can do far more than raise our awareness—for that in itself is not the whole picture—it can help us believe in ourselves, prompting a journey of self-discovery. Every occasion that we are near to a horse, an interaction takes place that we may or may not be aware of. When we open up to who and what the horse is, it can be quite a shock. For instead of "just" a four-legged animal observing us, we realize that someone super- sensitive and intelligent who *knows* us is by our side. The horse's way of getting directly down to the business in hand of being an open, direct, and honest communicator, means that as his or her disclosures dawn on us so, too, does an understanding of our identity and role in life. Eleanor found this out by simply being around horses, commenting:

> I am not a horsey person but a clinical psychologist who seems to have a gift in communication. Last year I ended up living with my daughter due to a family tragedy, helping out by feeding her eight horses. I found myself transfixed by their beautiful souls and the more time I spend with them, the more that I find myself totally in love with their majesty and presence. Although feeding eight horses a day is a lot of work, it was a discovery of joy and I look forward to my time with them. Each day in the presence of these amazing creatures is a gift of great magnitude. Somehow they seem to know that I have no expectations of them, no desire to ride or have them perform in any way. My horse friends have enriched my life greatly and all have found places in my heart.

Tom, on the other hand, needs to take a more active role to counterbalance the time he spends sitting behind a desk:

> After a hard day in the office I saddle my horse and ride until it gets dark. For a while my horse seems to understand that I need to unwind, then when I am ready, he also seems to know when to step up the pace, suddenly breaking into a canter. It always feels right, and I trust my horse to know how to look after me, and what I need when. We have no set routine on our rides, and that makes it great fun and it works very well because my horse and I are both free spirits yet in partnership . . . we know each other intimately. He has taught me about teamwork, a skill which has transferred across to other areas in my life.

Horses are sensitive and curious, both reasons why they interact with humans so well, but some find them intimidating and for them building a relationship with these animals can be challenging. However, people quickly discover that horses are not without feelings and reflect thoughts, emotions, and deeds. If we want to develop a meaningful relationship with horses, it means rekindling innate wisdom and moving away from objectifying them.

One challenge can be whether or not we are able to admit our own failings, for much is missed when we neglect to recognize the horse's unique contribution, not least that he or she holds a key to our education at the deepest level. Knowledge comes through our mistakes as well as when we do things right the first time and learning to care for a horse is both an art and a science. To gain a horse's trust and then accomplish tasks in spite of fears and lack of initial confidence, results in gaining skills that can be used to deal with other challenging situations that rely on our inner resources.

There is no end to our experiences with horses, only continual beginnings. Wisdom abounds in nature, including horse nature, which does not discriminate as to who to offer enlightenment to . . . it's there for anyone who needs help, and that's all of us.

Delving deep

Horses are not all things to all people—they frequently try to choose who they want to be with and can be fiercely loyal and committed partners. Whatever type of horse we connect with, he or she gets to share our secrets, hopes, laughter, and tears. In the barn or stable yard we can find sanctuary from an unsettled world, and this is also where priorities become clear as the horse presents us with reminders about what time spent away from the man-made world means. The horse brings us back to a fundamental place, valuing the most important things in life—food, water, shelter, freedom, reproduction, caring for offspring, and socializing with friends. These requirements underline the essential survival issues for the human race as well. The majority of our fears about the future revolve around these things; in this respect, therefore, we are not so different from horses and have every reason to share their concept of life.

We have become so entwined one with the other, that a measure of humanity's success is reflected in how we treat horses. Despite thousands of years of domestication, problems surrounding them are many. These include physical, mental, and emotional conditions due to incorrect weaning/handling/training/riding methods/tack/feeding and, of course, lifestyle. Problems reflect the fact that humans are not getting much right and there is an enormous debt owed. An important lesson often over-looked is that emotional and mental happiness are as vital to the phys-ical well-being of the horse as they are for us. In *Mental Health and Well-Being in Animals,* Franklin D. McMillan concludes that there is no longer any reasonable doubt among researchers that mental health is of equal importance as physical health in animal well-being. He states that research convincingly shows that physical health is strongly influenced by mental states, thereby making it clear that effective animal health care requires paying attention to emotional well-being as well as physical requirements. Before we present ourselves to horses saying, "Teach me all you know," we must first understand their own needs.

What do horses need?

All horses retain the physiology and anatomy of flight animals. They have evolved to be constantly on the move over large distances, eating lightly for most of the time—lifestyle elements essential for their all-around health. Mental/emotional/physical problems occur due to horses being kept inactive for long periods and fed high-protein diets with inter-vening periods of hunger. The energy from the sun, on which all life depends, is collected by plants during the process of photosynthesis. Such light-based energy is not only necessary for plants to live but for the animals that feed on them. Horses that are not allowed to graze natu-rally will be deprived of this essential form of vitality.

> "All horses are healers in their own individual way, and all horses want to help us to heal."

What matters to horses and how do they see the world?

To a horse, independence is an alien state: unsettling and depressing. In free-roaming and feral horses, their society is based on kinship, avoiding conflicts, and respecting each other's space. Aggressive interactions in domestic horses are mainly due to competition for water and food or due to restriction of space by humans.

A survival strategy in horses is forming long-term stable relation-ships. Within herds, equines have defined roles and behaviors, whereas in the domestic environment, the social group is constantly changing, resulting in high levels of anxiety and stress. This is reflected in training and schooling, the horse frequently getting the blame for not paying attention, being unpredictable or even dangerous, when actually he or she is deeply troubled.

21

Do horses connect with us in the same way that we think we do with them?

Through the horse's sense of awareness that everything is part of a whole, they interact with everything. Dramatic changes take place when we shift direction through understanding the perception of a horse, enabling us to connect to an emerging future and move away from a stagnant past. This means a shift for us personally, as well as in terms of our relationships with horses.

How do horses view the energy around them that comprises the world?

Horses, like all animals, read energy signals emanating from everything around them, including the energetic pulses and rhythms of the earth and other planets. Although humans exist within the same interplay, we have many blocks to awareness of the universal intelligence system, whereby all that there is interacts and communicates via an unseen level.

Most important of all, what can we give the horse, a species that gives us so much?

Through unconditional love we can strive to do the best for our equine partners.

Horses do not judge us or hold grudges, even though we may make them sad; as a species they seem to want humans to succeed, patiently waiting in the wings with unlimited pertinent wisdom and support. Many people respond to this by becoming passionate about horses and by paying homage to them in terms of their commitment, or through celebrating them with artistic endeavour.

Chain reaction

In every corner of the globe there are people who discover the potency of interacting with horses, including Gemma, whose pony came into her life at just the right time:

As a single parent with a young daughter, life has been very hard and I began to feel as though I was losing my way. Just when everything seemed hopeless I was asked to look after a five-year-old pony, Jazz, who was desperately in need of a home. He has received incredible care and love from us and from knowing absolutely nothing about horses I have discovered the most amazing world. Every day is a new experience. My daughter is now riding Jazz and he has *become* our daily lives. It's difficult to describe just how much Jazz has enriched our living, how much strength and support he gives us.

An all-round teacher

Most human teachers specialize in one particular topic, even those who work with horses. If people teach several things, the breadth of their subjects often becomes diluted and they can find themselves labeled "Jack of all trades, master of none." In order to learn experientially, we first need to have self-awareness and incredibly the horse can expertly teach anyone about him- or herself. Everyone appears to be looking for something different in life, even if the general themes may be similar, because human needs are as diverse as our personalities. Horses are a perfect match for undertaking this enormous task of broad-based teaching. Having the ability to be exactly what each person needs them to be, to be everything to everyone and at an exact moment in time, the horse is unsurpassed in an educational role and touched with brilliance. Each equine teaches us something different; just think of something that you need help with and you can be sure that one or more horses can open up avenues of learning that apply to your life. No matter what age group, class, culture, creed, or background you belong to, you can be a student of the horse. When the human has courage, humility and offers love, connection with horses is a never-ending continuum of education.

Human tutors can underperform and fail to adhere to standards. The horse, however, is consistent and his/her lessons are always of the highest quality. If they fail, it's because we are disengaged or not paying attention. The best pupils do not learn on their own terms alone—as a pupil the horse is naturally incapable of this way of being, due to listening continuously to input from everything and everyone. By following this initiative, we humans can gather and harness information to expand our horizons, taking on board as much as possible to elevate our thinking.

Not being able to teach a horse what we want him or her to learn is a completely different issue, because often the horse can't deduce any sense or benefit in what we ask. It always comes down to the same parameters . . . does it help the world, does it do the horse good, is it the right thing, does it improve quality of life, is it a soul-to-soul connection? If none or few of these things are true, horses surmise that it is us who are in need of a lesson, not them.

Beverly wrote to me with her story some time after watching one of my demonstrations. Something in the horse's response as I worked aroused in her a desire to leave her high-pressured office job and take courses in holistic horsemanship. Leaving the city for the last time she felt a sudden urge to look out of the train window and send healing to the many horses working in the city environment. Beverly told me that although she was leaving the rat race, the horses did not have a choice. Now a qualified instructor and trainer, she ended her letter by saying:

> I am in wonderment sometimes at how I've been able to map out my journey so far and have marveled at horses being the center of this. I feel strongly that horses are my future and that I am meant to work with them in some way. I know this because people and horses have led me to open doors that I've felt encouraged to go through.

Jane described her relationship with a black mare called Duchess:

> I own a horse who is teaching me all that she knows. Mentally and physically worn down from numerous operations I realized that my horse needed me as much as I did her, and I had to be fit to care for her. I have not been ill now for years . . . I only feel completely well and myself when I am with my horse. Things have not always gone according to plan, but I love her without reservation.

Sue, who had started riding after being widowed in her early forties, reiterates what horse lovers the world over feel about their relationships: "Blue is in my head all day, every day. I never stop thinking about him and what he has revealed to me. He seems to be a powerful unique friend that has changed my life in a very short space of time."

Feeling alive

There is a mystery to horses, yet at the same time they can also feel very familiar to us. This is something that I get frequent comments about and typical is Judy's expression of her connection with her horse Orion: "He was not what I was looking for, but I fell in love when I saw him. I adore him. I dream of him night and day and he has rejuvenated my life."

Carolyne is an accountant and early each morning she attends to her horses before going back home to change into a business suit ready for her commute to work, returning to the yard in the evening. Her partner suggested she employ someone to do the morning shift to give her more time for herself, but Carolyne refused, explaining, "It's the best bit of the day and sets me up for my time in the office."

Despite being seriously ill in the hospital following a complicated reaction to prescription medication, Tara insisted on being taken to see her horses. At the time, the doctors didn't know what was wrong with Tara, and thought that maybe she had had a stroke or a brain tumor, but they agreed to the horse visits because anything that lifted her spirits was worth trying. Technically, Tara should have found the trips exhausting, but they had quite the opposite effect—in fact, she found that spending time with the horses was uplifting, making her feel much better and increasing her energy levels. Later, when Tara's mare tragically died leaving a distraught five-week foal, she faced a real responsibility and challenge. There was no hiding or quitting option and instead of crying into a pillow Tara had to be with the foal every few hours to nurse her through the summer. She survived and was a healing influence on Tara, who told me that this little scrap of life carried her through her own very difficult time.

I remember once meeting a colleague for lunch and for the first hour or so as we discussed ideas her face was taut. We decamped to a comfy sofa to let our meal digest, when I suddenly realized that my associate looked years younger as an inner beauty lit her features. When I remarked on this she said, "I feel like I've come alive now that we are talking about horses." It reminded me of the first time my husband watched me give healing to a horse, remarking afterward, "You were a completely different person"—someone he almost did not recognize. Luckily he did not feel offended, acknowledging that a unique connection, on another level to relationships with humans, was responsible for my transformation. Daily, people the world over experience this magnificent phenomenon.

> "The horse becomes part of you, your destiny. Even when daily contact is broken, you are still part of an eternal connection."

Why not cats or dogs?

Undoubtedly there are life lessons to be learned from all animals, especially whales, dolphins, and elephants, but these animals are not readily accessible to everyone, nor can the majority of us have them in our day-to-day lives. Available in most areas, though, horses can teach all races and cultures about responsibility, hard work, communication, patience, relationships, and caring. It has become accepted that the horse's way of mirroring energies provides opportunities for metaphorical learning.

25

Horses are playful individuals with distinct individual personality traits, moods, attitudes, and behaviors and, in that respect, they challenge our own temperament and behaviors.

Unlike most pets, horses are big animals that live outside the home, making us experience the elements through our involvement with them. They are also unpredictable and may develop problems that can be difficult to diagnose. For a satisfying relationship with horses we are required to put in a great deal of effort and input, and in this era of self-gratification that in itself can be a hard lesson to learn. Moreover, we have to engage in mental and emotional work, and this, in turn, leads to self-development.

Like humans, cats and dogs are predators and hunters. A predatory life means having an independent approach, and the need to go off and act in a selfish way. If there is a meal going that you have to catch, while the cat or dog may act partly in a pack mode, the desire to get food selfishly overrides any other external commands. Horses get eaten by other animals but do not hunt them down. Being herbivores, they eat while being constantly alert to potential attack. Dogs, and to some extent cats, can be trained, rewarded, and coerced to do things by using food. This does not work with horses due to overriding stimuli telling them whether to stay or move away. Only when we become a real leader can we encourage them to follow our instructions.

Understanding prey and predator

The willingness of horses to be with humans involves far more than a mere submission to us as predators. Ethologist and horse-human relationship specialist Mary Ann Simonds states:

> The scientific model we have used for generations teaches that horses are a prey species and humans are predators. However, in more modern approaches, especially from an evolutionary consciousness perspective, humans have the ability to mirror or reflect any species they choose. Underlying all scientific models is the reality that humans can choose to match the energy of the animal they are with and use an empathic approach.
>
> Horses are not so black and white to view us as predators. In fact, with the exception of wild horses, most horses view us as other social mammals. When we chase them around in circles then the prey/predator may apply, however, when we use horse language such

as spatial awareness, we are then connecting to horses in their terms, and this is viewed as how social mammals make friendships and establish leadership. The foundation for functional horse culture is the ability to form strong social bonds. The good leaders in both equine and human societies have the ability to clearly communicate and make friends with everyone.

> 66 I didn't just buy a sad horse from a dealer's field, I bought a whole life change, which has given me the opportunity to meet like-minded spiritual people. I'm really grateful for that. 99
> *Emma, carer of Jazz*

Horses truly understand species interdependence, even though humans can be uncooperative in this area, and there are social equilibrium commonalities between us. Both humans and horses are group animals, with hierarchical and social structures, which need to be stable for overall well-being and survival. There is often something that we cannot actually identify in the horse but, lacking a better description, we can call it the horse's spiritual nature. Humankind is inherently a spiritual animal but frequently out of touch with spirituality. It is this quality in horses that attracts many people to spend time with them, as well as the fact that they resonate with the cooperative, non-predatory form of power that horses reflect.

The horse has never lost its way. Perhaps the horse is our alter ego and that is why, when with them, we are encouraged to reflect on who we are in order to become complete. I believe that the horse has chosen to do this for us; the mystery is what lies beyond the here and now that makes it a vital and pressing journey to take.

People have often posed the question to me: what is it about horses that invokes such a strong response in humans, such that they can have a transformational effect on a person's life? My answer is that they are messengers of hope and the embodiment of pure sacred love; that is what nurtures us.

Alignment

While writing this book I was introduced to author, dressage judge, and coach Wendy Jago at a workshop incorporating horses to encourage business delegates to explore ideas from a new perspective. It was wonderful to be able to discuss our mutual passion and what we can learn from horses. I asked Wendy what she felt that the connection was that made the horse such a powerful catalyst for change in people. What is "a healing horse"? Wendy gave me this profound statement:

The horse aligns us with ourselves across all levels, including thinking, feeling, and being. Unless damaged in some way, horses are congruent with themselves, and if we are not, then there is a challenge to our misalignment. The challenge offers us an invitation because it shows us what can be possible when we are comfortable within. On the whole, horses are contented within themselves—being a horse. Maybe this invites us to consider how we can be at ease within *ourselves*, even though we have our limitations.

When we take on board the logic of this concept, we can begin to realize just why the horse is far more than a vehicle to move us around, look good on, or just be a means to winning competitions. Horses speak to us, continually offering feedback, and that not only includes information about our world but about theirs too.

2 The cosmic horse

Horses are an enigma. Direct and simplistic in their approach, yet simultaneously complex, they are sophisticated and sensitive beings capable of reading humans intimately on the deepest level. No wonder so many people become smitten by them. We marvel at their size, power, and strength and try hard to understand them, a defining moment being when we realize that the horse is a spiritual entity.

Finding what our essential non-material needs are comes from investigating territory above and beyond everyday reality, and in this process we can be guided by many different messengers. When, and if, we are ready, the horse can open up for us experiences of incredible depth, affording us access to a unique inner capacity to serve the information that emerges. While considering the qualities of horses as guides to exploration, it came to me that the term "cosmic horse" aptly describes their special attributes. Tapping into the cosmic community, the horse invites us into a landscape where we can find direction, exploring how we need to be in order to reach affinity with not only ourselves but all life-forms.

My interpretation of this approach is that it is also about becoming aware of synchronicity and universal messages, since the horse picks up energy that the explorer emits and reflects it. I am convinced that the horse is entirely complicit in this exercise and enjoys the good humor and newfound respect the explorer gives as insights are received. It is a unique partnership—a connection arising from the spirit of the horse. The cosmic horse is potentially any horse: all have something to teach and as we go through life we will partake in many varied encounters. To reap the benefit of what unfolds, it's important to have a desire to learn and understand more than we already do. Aristophanes, an ancient Greek writer, summed it up by saying that, "teaching doesn't mean filling empty vessels but kindling a fire." Once that fire—a desire to improve—is burning inside us it can never be extinguished, and as we travel our pathway, the fuel that can keep it going is the commitment of horses. They care about you and me, and whether our heart and soul are wounded or healed.

The horse is a symbolic representation of the higher self and our deepest passions. This is why the horse is emerging as an amazing link between our conscious and subconscious mind, and the mysterious source of all life. A relationship with a horse enables us to consider the concepts of the higher self (soul level) and the conditioned self (money, status, power). The horse has full understanding of the former, but no inkling of the latter—except to show us clearly when the energy generated from the attitude of the conditioned self is unhealthy. As well as being a healer, the horse is a catalyst for getting in touch with our inner healer, from where moments of inspiration stem.

As part of the growing numbers of those seeking enlightenment, more and more horse carers, trainers, riders, and instructors are seeking to explore and understand the spiritual talents of the horse. Where once the words "spirituality" and "horse" would not have been uttered in the same breath there is now nothing unusual about that link. Spirituality is a perception and an understanding of inner worlds. It is about being open to dialogue with the World Soul and thus intermingling and blending to oneness with the souls of all creatures.

Spiritual thinking and encounters are personal and outside of the boundaries of religion. In order to mean anything, true spirituality has to be an experience and not just be a concept. Therefore, it has to manifest itself through something tangible that we can relate to in our everyday lives. Horses have incredible potential as spiritual beacons and are frequently described as "divine mirrors" for their ability to stimulate enlightened thinking. Many people, myself included, believe that horses understand spiritual achievements because they sense energies within us and know when a shift has taken place at even the deepest soul level. Anecdotal evidence is a testament to this, whereby people frequently describe improvements in their relationships with horses when they themselves become more spiritually aware.

Horses offer us vision, based on listening to our core instincts. They can assist us to expand our horizons by observing and exploring feelings, ideas, and senses, to rise above the everyday and mundane. It is not just rhetoric or theory; it has become a reality for thousands of horse carers and riders. It is the reason why around the world horses are increasingly becoming guides and facilitators in work such as coaching, education, psychotherapy, rehabilitation, and experiential learning. Horses effortlessly demonstrate and embody "living in the present"—a fundamental spiritual teaching. The awareness that we can achieve through this also helps our relationships with other people: imagine what a wonderful world it would be if all humans listened to the horse!

> **❝**Imagine what a wonderful world it would be if all humans listened to the guidance and wisdom on offer from the horse.**❞**

A liberating process

Horses are so much more adept at interpreting the levels of reality than we are because we can become sidetracked, restricting our inner growth. This can happen on many levels, including our awareness, understanding, and emotional development. Connecting with a horse is a liberating process in itself, inviting us to set aside any preconceived ideas or indoctrinations that we may hold.

> "For many years," admits Sue from Scotland, "I was bound into fundamentalist thinking but became increasingly aware of its limitations and hold on me, particularly regarding my animals and sense of oneness with the natural world, until I realized that I wasn't in touch with myself. However, when something is true, it has a habit of catching up with you and finally I became emancipated by listening to horses. I look forward to each new day with an almost stomach-churning excitement at what my horses are going to tell me and teach me, also what I can give back to them. At last I am coming into the real me. All this success from someone who for years was plagued with low moods and was an eternal pessimist. My gratitude is heartfelt."

Stepping out of any type of restriction that creates a false identity, into the intuitive powerhouse of the natural world, can stimulate and encourage us to become our authentic selves, rather than a product of someone else's ideology. How wonderful it is that in tandem with horses we can be stimulated to do this.

Teamwork

From time to time we may witness something so moving that it evokes very strong emotion. Such an event occurred as I watched a film of six women rescuing nearly one hundred and fifty Fresian horses stranded on a tiny island in the Netherlands after a storm sea flood. Several horses had already died and a giant rescue operation was discussed; however, the use of boats and helicopters was ruled out as they would most likely have frightened the horses, causing more to drown. There were horses of all ages and their distress reached out to me even though I was watching the images on my computer.

Six women on horseback appeared on the shore; their horses waiting for action as they faced the stranded herd. Suddenly, four of the riders plowed into the water, their mounts striding forward with a wonderfully flamboyant high-stepping action. On and on they went, the water varying in depth, causing them to swim every now and again.

The moment when they reached the stranded horses had me in tears, for their body language seemed to say, "You have come to save us." The cosmic resonance binding together the people and the horses was both palpable and haunting. The riders then turned to head back home and there followed an intense moment as, one by one, the stricken horses followed until a long line snaked through the water, the ridden horses leading the way through the currents. Splashing water was interspaced with hollering as the riders and people on land encouraged the rescued horses to the shore. Some were making a better job of it than others; the old, foals, and the weak falling into and then struggling through the hidden channels, quite deep in places. The ridden horses did not waiver as they led the herd to safety until each one arrived on dry land to be checked by vets, dried, fed, and watered.

Susan was one of the two riders who stayed by a wall to help direct the herd when they arrived on dry land:

> It was a very emotional moment, really beautiful. I can't describe how it is when one hundred and fifty horses are running towards you. My horse was a little bit scared I must admit, but he was great; when the horses ran past him there was a moment when I lost control but then he was OK about it all. The most beautiful moment was when the four horses entered the water to go to the stranded horses and my horse wanted to go with them. I said to him, "No, you cannot go, we must stay here as a backup." Then my horse made some noises, calling to the horses that had gone into the water. They made the same noises back to him and that touched my heart.

Horses are in their element when together in a herd, and teamwork is also what can bring out the best in human nature. When we experience the helping energy of social groups it becomes a healing connection. In today's world, humans have become isolated from each other, with families and groups of friends (our herd) becoming fragmented. We all need to feel that our contribution is valued, but the breakdown of communities means we have little chance to be of service. It is becoming a lost art to feel settled, especially spiritually, and people do need to feel that they fit in somewhere. For many, horses help them integrate into society, providing opportunities for communal participation in a common interest. Through this connection, people can learn a lot about organizational abilities and how to engage more actively, enabling them to become aware of the details of their experiences.

Horses isolated from the herd become depressed and resentful, in the same way that we do through an unfulfilled longing to be part of a social group. I knew a woman who deliberately kept a horse on his own until she realized that it was a reflection of her bitterness, sustaining her loneliness. The day she put him into a herd and heard his call of joy, she felt released from her exile. A week later, one of the horse owners introduced her to a friend who she soon married. Her horse was guest of honor at the wedding, pulling the carriage that took her to the church.

A sense of humor

A sense of *joie de vivre* is acknowledged to be a mood enhancer boosting the immune system and being outdoors is also proven to raise the spirits. A study carried out by Essex University for the charity Mind found that after a country walk many of those who took part reported decreased levels of depression, felt less tense and also increased self-esteem. Sharing a walk with a horse has similar therapeutic benefits. Horses generally encourage us to have fun in many ways and, on many occasions, they have impressed me with their sense of humor.

It was the end of a busy week and I finished it by visiting a friend who was having a few problems with a pony called Barney. Amy told me that for some reason the pony did not like her, although he was OK with her daughter and the girl who rode him. Barney had lived with Amy for a couple of years and then Amy had found what she thought to be a good home for him elsewhere. All seemed to go well but after six months he went lame and Amy took him back. Her vet then found a few health problems and it transpired that the new home had not been so good after all.

It was difficult for me to get any information from Barney at first but as he relaxed the atmosphere changed and I asked him again why he did not like Amy. "She smells," he said. I was shocked . . . she was standing next to me and there was no odor that I could detect, but then I am not a horse and have less sensitive senses. "Meat . . . she smells of meat," he explained. I felt that this could not be correct as I knew Amy to be a vegetarian. Tactfully I broached the topic and was very surprised when Amy admitted to having recently eaten a large amount of meat. I explained that for Barney a human who smelled of ingesting meat reminded him that the person was a predator who could eat him too. It is one of the reasons that I do not eat meat myself and Amy apologized, telling the pony that she would cease immediately. Barney then communicated that he was angry

> **"**The energetic sensation of riding a horse has no comparison; when we feel as one, it's the most magical connection, not just with the horse, but the whole universe.**"**

with Amy for sending him away and he was glad to be back.

"I know that he is angry with me about that," Amy said, tears welling up in her eyes, "but I have never done anything else bad to him."

I heard laughter coming from Barney's direction, followed by him saying, "Oh yes, you have." Oh dear, I thought, whatever is coming next; then I heard him say, "You gave me a boiled sweet . . . it was awful, I hated it."

When I conveyed this to Amy she started to laugh, clutching her sides with mirth until the tears of sadness became tears of joy. This was so infectious we all joined in the laughter, not knowing what the joke was about. When Amy told us we roared. A couple of weeks before, when Barney had pulled a face at Amy, she had thought to herself, *What can I do to encourage him to like me? I know, I'll offer him a treat.* Rummaging in her pockets she found a mint-flavored sweet, which she had unwrapped and offered to Barney, who took it into his mouth. The pony then promptly spat out the lozenge before turning his back and walking away.

Barney appeared to be smiling, one corner of his upper lip curled up and his eyes twinkled. The horse had had his say, all was forgiven and now he was healing us with laughter, teaching us that we should not take everything too seriously. The good humor certainly did lift our mood, ending our week on a high note.

The cosmic horse

Cosmic *adj*
Of the universe or cosmos.

Horse *n & v*
Solid-footed, plant-eating quadruped, Equus caballas, with flowing mane and tail, used for riding and to carry and pull loads.

Cosmic horse
A horse that helps us to connect to the very heart of the universe and all that there is. Teacher, healer, and friend.

All equines are of the cosmos and all are equally valid as healer and teacher. We should not overlook one in preference to another in case we miss a vital lesson or piece of information. It's important to honor all equine gifts because they are a gateway to understanding the infinite, and collectively they are a bridge to our cosmic home, which they have never left.

Generous spirit

There are times when I feel like a horse, but for the wrong reasons. After too long being confined to my office I feel disconnected from nature, which affects my equilibrium, and horses are my medicine for such ailments.

Piper, a stunning pale blond Arab, reminded me of the unstinting generosity of horses. Five years previously Piper had been in a barn fire, the roof having fallen in around him, and since then the horse had been afraid of doorways, rushing through and sometimes falling as a result. One such incident resulted in the horse having a year off ridden work to recover from his injuries and the previous owners had not been kind to him. However, he was eager to meet me, pushing his nose into my hands before I touched him all over to help soothe his physical and emotional discomfort through healing energy. The horse oozed love and was very chatty, transmitting sensations and images to me of his past life, flowing from his mind to mine like an intense kaleidoscope of color.

Piper brightened up considerably as time passed, until with a huge sigh, the horse went to eat, pushing the groom aside to reach the hay, a very good sign as he had recently not been eating too well. After a few minutes he came back and rested the tip of his nose on the groom's arm and in that moment I sensed an image suspended between them, a picture of the groom holding a cat in her arms, and with it a feeling of concern from the horse. I asked the groom if she knew what this meant and she explained that two days previously her cat had suddenly become ill, and it was at the vet's that she had cradled him. He was thankfully OK now, but how did the horse know what had happened?

I asked Piper; he reminded me that horses know everything about us, and at all times. Piper liked the groom because she was gentle and empathic, and despite the traumas that Piper had gone through and his own need, offered healing support to her. Generosity of spirit is what the cosmic horse is all about. This experience reminded me again that a relationship with a horse can be extraordinarily complex yet also very explicit. It's a matter of simply "being" and the horse will do the rest.

Other nations

Over the past hundred years or so, technology has grown beyond our wildest imaginings and new inventions continuously appear. This has given the human race unbridled power; however, wisdom and enlightenment have not grown at the same pace and the unabated troubles that

The famous horse

Some years after Desert Orchid, one of the most famous racehorses of all time, retired from the track, I came into contact with him and was astounded by the air of supernatural energy and authority that the handsome grey exuded. After the horse died at the grand age of twenty-seven, I spoke with his co-owner Midge Burridge, who told me of the extraordinary healing effect that the horse had had on people. When those who were sick, incapacitated, or depressed met Dessie, as the horse was nicknamed, they would afterward report feeling better. Thousands wrote to Midge about this phenomenon, extolling Dessie's healing virtues.

Desert Orchid was a big, strong horse, full of vitality even in old age, yet in the presence of the vulnerable, frail or children he was extremely gentle. One day a friend of Midge's family, who had spent years in a wheelchair with multiple sclerosis, announced that she was going to get out of her chair and walk over to where the horse was standing . . . and she was motivated to do just that. As the woman shakily reached Dessie, he calmly lowered his head, enabling her to fold her arms around his neck and hug him, soaking up the strength of the horse's powerful essence.

> **"** Horses always know whether someone is coming from a place of self-interest or operating through compassion, an essential quality to have. **"**

people encounter are testament to this. We have reached a critical moment in evolution and the fact that we need to take stock is reflected in the stressed state that the earth has reached. Exploitation and neglect have taken their toll as mankind has lost touch with, and manipulated, the forces of nature.

Resolution can be found by listening to horse sense, which has nothing high tech about it yet is succinct and to the point. However, humankind is not a magnanimous species when it comes to sharing the earth with other creatures. Central to human development and domination of the earth is our need to view humans as above and beyond every other creature. This assumption allows humans to deny sentience, intelligence, love, and joy in animals so that they can go about their lives secure in the knowledge that no animal is suffering at their expense. Accepting that animals have the right to live according to their natural laws will be resisted as long as possible because it means a revision of conscience regarding non-human animal treatment.

We are all co-inhabitants and as far as the cosmos is concerned—the hub of reality—humans are not more privileged as a species than any other. Non-human animals are not beneath us, despite having been placed in that position by a worldview, but exist as nations in their own right, and we need to adopt a more knowledgeable comprehension of their role. There is a paradigm shift taking place as scientists are increasingly acknowledging that animals are much more complex than they had previously realized. There is also evidence that animals accept as normality extensions of the senses that humans have either lost or never had. As well as operating and communicating through the sixth sense, they have a wider range of hearing, sight, and sense of smell. Their senses also extend to picking up magnetic and electrical fields. I have found that by viewing horses as a nation, not "just" animals, my awareness has been empowered enormously and, quite honestly, I could not do my work without that premise.

Erecting barriers between ourselves and animals means living with a blind spot and operating naively, resulting in missed opportunities for personal development. Around the world, people are realizing that horses are able to rekindle and then integrate a deep understanding, and this may take place when riding, handling, or simply standing near to them. Jan, a nurse, had such an awakening:

> Brushing my horse's mane I suddenly felt as though we were both connected to a single intelligence, then with a sort of "whoosh" we blended into one person. I can only describe the sensation as like sharing the same mind, and for a moment I was filled with a wisdom that was alien to me. It was a sensational feeling and I wanted to hold onto it forever because I thought what phenomenal good it would do for my patients.

Businessman James described:

> ...a moment out riding when I heard what my horse was thinking ...thoughts entering my mind which I knew were not my own, because they were from the perspective of a horse. For a long time I was afraid to tell anyone in case they thought I was crazy. However, I have since come across others who also pick up messages from horses and I now believe it to be a type of normality. It has changed the way that I deal with people in that it's dawned on me that none of us operates in isolation, even if we think we do.

Horses are a nation of horse-shaped entities keying into the network of universal consciousness or intelligence. Because of this, horses hold a position from where they have an overview of totality; we can make much of the benefit this offers us.

3 Exploring connections

No matter what our concept of horses, when in their proximity, we are connected to them through fields of energy. Within that connection are varying levels of communication and understanding. There is a continuous analytical process taking place from the horse's perspective, which leads us to an adventure in consciousness.

The term "connection" is used frequently in the horse world as a means of measuring how we get on with a particular horse. Trainers, instructors, and workshop leaders use this word to explain that to link with the horse we need to be open to feedback. The presence we project is instrumental to good communication and, on the whole, horses are more aware of the human energetic presence than humans are of the horse's. However, presence is far more than a momentary union. It is about allowing an emergence of information that we would not normally be aware of, increasing the scope of our knowledge beyond normal preconceptions. This means that instead of making assumptions or following routines, we find we have access to a more pertinent level of existence. Connection can take place irrespective of whether we ride, care for a horse, or have a fleeting contact.

Horses look for authenticity in order for them to want to connect with us. Authenticity can be defined as being keyed into our energetic presence, correlating and amalgamating inner and outer emotional states, without conflict at any of those levels. When authenticity is expressed, we are able to "see" the horse within and from within ourselves.

Unlike humans, horses are unwilling to accept incongruence of any sort as it takes them into a state of agitation. Humans frequently pick up inconsistent information from others; it's just that we often either ignore it or don't act on it. For my own part, whenever I do either, I get into a mess, making me resolve that I must always follow the horse's example by discharging what I feel rather than letting it sit with me as an unwanted burden.

41

Ebb and flow

There are different levels of connection, sometimes fluctuating and other times holding fast. Even if we are fully aware, it can feel like watching the ebb and flow of the tide, as one minute things seem to be going well, then suddenly they go awry. Louise, studying horse management, found this with a horse called Sonny who did not trust people, due to past abuse: "Some days I thought that I had connected with Sonny, albeit only briefly. I show my fear easily and was wary of going near the horse so as not to upset him. One day I decided to sit in the field watching him and when I got up he followed me as if there was some sort of connection between us. Since this event I have found it easy to ride him, yet he is violent towards other people." All relationships are unique and need continuous work to keep them harmonious. It's a question of constantly listening, offering love and being open to see which horse will want to bond with us . . . hopefully all of them!

> If we seek a 'perfect horse,' we first need to be a perfect human.

Decisions

There are many reasons why we may or may not relate to a horse. Our thoughts and feelings, although hidden from others, are constantly tuned into by the equine radar and the bar to closeness may therefore be created by what is happening within *us*. However, if there are issues, then equine pain and illness must always be eliminated for we are not going to have the best connection possible with a horse that is not happy with life. Each horse will have limitations, just as we do, and our expectations should not be inflexible. As with any relationship, if expectations are unrealistic, we are prone to being disappointed. When we are adaptive, life offers endless adventures, as Lin discovered:

This morning we went out for a ride, the first in five weeks due to the lambing season and my dog having puppies. It was not long and at a gentle pace, but on the way out we had to pass a truck unloading a tractor mower with big suction tubes. Rowan didn't like it very much but nevertheless continued. As we returned, the mower was making a huge noise and hitting stones. Rowan hesitated, then spun around to head in the other direction. Rather than have a confrontation I decided to make a detour back home, a longer route, but after we had gone a short distance Rowan stopped, then turned back towards the noisy machine. Patting his neck I sensed that he wanted to go past, so I let him have his way. I was absolutely amazed because without any encouragement from me, he walked by the machine as if saying to me, "Come on, we can do it." I feel such a connection with him that I did not think would be possible.

Lack of confidence or fear can hold us back and, of course, we must always be aware of safety issues that the horse may not consider. When partnered with trust, horses have the opportunity to show facets of being able to look after us. All we need to do is absorb and feel, and interpretation of the horse's vision becomes accessible. Horses express purposefulness acted upon in the present moment, which can lead us to developing our own synchronicity of emotion and thought. Ultimately this leads to unison, one with the other.

Touch

The horse likes to be touched and herd cohesiveness is reinforced by mutual grooming. Many people never really touch their horses, only throwing tack or rugs on or brushing them. It's important to horses that we get into the habit of gentle hand grooming to help induce calmness and reinforce relationships. Research into touch and racehorses has produced evidence to show that when they were touched before the start of a race, stereotypical stress behaviors were dramatically reduced.

However, just like us, horses do like to be consulted before they are touched, so that it becomes a gift rather than an intrusion. I watched a class in which a couple of instructors were placing colored stickers onto a horse to demonstrate muscles and movement. Every now and then one would stop talking, go over to the horse, slap a sticker somewhere on him and each time the horse, alarmed, looked around at his body to try to make sense of what was going on. It was very disrespectful. All the couple had to do was show the stickers to the horse, explain what they were intending and why, and the horse would have said, "That's OK, I will help you teach today." Connection includes honoring another's feelings, no matter what species, and not least because their bodies belong to them.

> 66 When we ignore energy, we miss 99 percent of reality. 99

Intention

Horses and ponies have much to teach us about the meaning of intention, which can be defined as an aim or resolution to make something happen. Intention has a very powerful energy of its own and has an objectiveness attached to it, but it is not the same thing as desire. Desire involves focusing on what we want to happen, an outcome. Our wishes, hopes, and desires have an independent energy that transforms the nature of our world, with thoughts continuously manifesting as our reality. This means that if we think negatively, we invite things to go wrong and our fears become self-fulfilling.

Having positive intentions helps us to achieve goals. Sometimes we are not aware of our intentions, which can become buried inside us, often leading to frustration when a horse does not respond to our wishes as to what we want him or her to do. In areas of challenge we need to ask ourselves, "What was I actually thinking when the situation went wrong? What do I learn from this?" It means directing energy at the intender's own thoughts and actions, shifting expectations and reasoning, as happened with Cheryl. She had contacted me in desperation after her injured horse became distressed at being treated by her, and she, in turn, became upset at this. In the end, both became nervous wrecks, but I knew that by changing her thoughts, Cheryl could break the cycle.

She explained: "After crying in frustration this morning I really focused on my own positive thinking. Lo and behold, in the right frame of mind I was able to clip the lead rope on calmly and put ointment into the eye. We had a cuddle and then off I went. After the ever-increasing battles and worries of the last few days it was a wonderfully panic- and fear-free experience."

Due to their understanding of energy form, horses are adept mind readers, perceiving our intentions as instructions. By learning to convey what we really want as an outcome, we can eliminate our fears and uncertainties from the mutual dialogue. We can imagine, formulate, and demonstrate, creating ideas that can take us onto a new pathway or territory, or which may only ever live in our minds but are powerful energy instructions nevertheless. A thought therefore is an actual "something," which will have an impact on how any animal will behave with us, horses in particular.

The power of thought is recognized by the scientific community and is already used to control artificial limbs. In recognizing the potential of intention, scientists are hoping to produce thought-activated TVs and other equipment. Another technique called optical topography reads thoughts by measuring changes in blood flow to key areas of the brain. These changes, detected in a sensor cap worn by the "thinker," are passed to a small computer, which decodes the signal, working out the person's intention, which then triggers a remote control to operate the desired piece of equipment.

Horses do not need such complicated technology for what they already do very well in this respect. The energy of thought exists; horses accept it and it is part of their language. However, because thought forms are invisible, on the whole, humans ignore the benefits or the repercussions of them.

If our intention is not honorable or is self-serving, horses will know it and the relationship falters. When a young woman asked me why she could not *make* her horse do what she wanted, I explained it was because the horse read her intention as bullying and would wish to avoid interaction. Changing the nature of her intention to *inviting* the horse to do certain things was in line with horse language and, not surprisingly, the feedback was that her horse had become amenable and that she had learned something valuable about her manner. Responses we get from horses have a direct correlation to our attitude, even if we try to hide it from the rest of the world.

Getting it together

One of the main reasons why people find it difficult to tune into their horses is due to a lack of focus. This blocks out the creative part of our nature, which we need to give space to in order to be perceptive.

Pinocchio, a show pony, impressed upon his rider Lyn that what she *intended* to happen was not being formulated as *intention*. Lyn had asked if I could throw some light on why the pony lacked sparkle (the vet had given him a clean bill of health). My conversation with him got off to a bizarre start when Pinocchio indicated that he liked punctuality. I started to think about Lyn's timekeeping but was quickly led to understand that the pony meant the timeliness of her thoughts with actions. He described being able to pick up what Lyn was gathering in her mind but then there followed a gap while she considered her options, so he became bored and switched off from the process. Pinocchio wanted a more direct approach, in keeping with the way of the horse, so I suggested that when Lyn wanted to trot, for example, she should intend it to happen there and then. Putting this newfound knowledge into practice resulted in Pinocchio responding with sparkle to the instantaneous rapport.

Strong intention requires focused purpose and projection of awareness; this the horse can relate to.

> 66 Touching a horse is connecting with the whole universe. 99

Intention and connection go hand in hoof

Intention has been described as being like a tuning fork, causing the energy of other entities in the universe to resonate with the same frequency. Resonance is harmonization at a multitude of levels. Through emotional resonance it's possible for anyone to unite with horses, for it has the integrity of interspecies coherence.

Intention is different from attention, but both are interlinked. The horse is attentive to our intention; therefore, it is vital to be aware of the powerful energy movement this triggers. Horses also have intentions of their own and when in herds can comply with them.

Intention in terms of building a meaningful relationship with a horse cannot be possession orientated; that, in itself, does not provide anything to connect with because human wishes and desires hold no interest. What does interest the horse is energy that has a synchronicity with the universe, such as positive loving thoughts of wanting to help and heal. This has an energetic form that horses understand and which attracts their attention.

Through intention we become energy co-creators of our world. It does not mean getting our own way; rather it's about generating dynamic qualities, appealing to others.

State of mind affects the quality of intention, which is why there are varying effects. Intention is an application that can be learned, rather than being a special or exclusive gift.

Directed intention manifests as both magnetic and electrostatic energy, and some people are naturally better at focusing their minds than others. Practice leads to a stronger mind–cosmos connection.

The signals we send out may not be what we think they are and this is why it is important to focus on thoughts so that we harness them rather than let them run riot and take control. Horses are very sensitive to cues from us, which can be so subtle that another human would not notice them, and our unspoken intentions will influence a horse's behavior and mood.

The broadcasting of good intent is not just received by a horse we are interacting with but registers with the whole universe as a beneficial energy. Potentially from that moment on, the rapport that we have with other beings is enhanced. Sometimes this occurs subtly, sometimes in a dramatic way, but there is always an awakening.

The leaf experiment

Thoughts and intentions are tangible energies and a growing number of scientific studies have quantified how energy generated from emotional, mental, and spiritual wishes influences both living and non-living systems. Professor William Braud of the Institute of Transpersonal Psychology, California, has shown that human thoughts can prevent the breakdown of cells in a laboratory, control the direction that fish swim, and make gerbils run faster on activity wheels. Healers use intention as a means of sending positive thoughts to help improve the health of patients, including animals, even if they have not met them, and animals are capable of effective intention towards each other.

During an investigation set up by Lynne McTaggart, author of *The Intention Experiment*, four hundred delegates from a London conference sent intention to the University of Arizona, Tucson, thousands of miles away. A team headed by consciousness researcher Dr. Gary E. Schwartz selected two leaves from a flourishing geranium plant and placed them under a webcam. The London audience selected which leaf to send their intention to, namely to make it glow. The scientific team did not know which leaf had been chosen and for ten minutes the audience sent their thought to the chosen leaf displayed on a giant screen; the results were expected to take weeks to analyze but the leaf glowed so brightly it was visible to the naked eye. This shows that we can indeed tune into others from a distance and powerfully influence their way of being. Wherever we are, if we are concerned about a horse or a person, we can send healing intention to help them "glow." It means, too, that when we say, "I'm thinking of you," this really does have a benefit.

> 66 The horse, like us, is an expression of the life within and only when we offer authentic connection will the horse offer friendship. 99

Developing effective intention skills

1 *Healing and meditation are the best ways to hone intention skills because both raise levels of awareness.*

2 *To open up our psychological boundaries for intention to work, empathy, self-belief, compassion, and concentration are vital components, all of which mean being fully aware of the other being.*

3 *The power of intention can be enhanced when a group of like-minded people get together to tune into a person or horse. You can use this technique to "power up" at any time. Asking for a specific result will not work, but sending love and best wishes will be most beneficial and can produce amazing results.*

4 *Offering a horse the intention of wanting to do the best that you possibly can encourages him or her to bond and join up with you.*

Disconnection

There are times when we can feel out of synch with a horse, and equally as many times, if not more, when horses feel disconnected from humans. Many factors affect relationships including our moods, hang-ups, health, the weather, and other people's influences. Someone may not even be aware she or he is not in harmony. On rather too many occasions I have seen people plow on regardless with a situation (including handling, training, riding, treating with therapies or veterinary medicine), when the problem stemmed from an initial lack of resonance between themselves and a horse. That may not be picked up on by clients and students who, using the same techniques, perpetuate the cycle of lack of understanding.

On one occasion I watched a demonstration by a trainer who had been brought a colt that reacted violently to having a halter put on. Confidently, the man explained his routine for fitting one. As he talked, the colt was jumping nervously around the center of the pen, staring in horror at the faces peering in. Half an hour later the trainer was no nearer getting the halter on the horse; every time he lifted his hand to slide it up the horse's neck, the horse started to rear and I sensed that the problem was a sore poll area. On pointing it out, the trainer commented, "It doesn't matter why a horse doesn't want to do something, he has to comply with what I want. Even if he has given up and wants me to stop, I will carry on until I get the result." When such total disconnection with a horse is prevailing, you get a miserable and confused horse, as stood before us that day, and a human who is barking up the wrong tree. One-and-a-half hours later, the spectators had gone elsewhere and the trainer gave up; the sweating, headachy colt had a rope thrown around his neck and was led away.

Another trainer and riding teacher gave a clinic in which several horses were brought in and let loose, and after they had all established contact with each other the woman walked towards the group. Being inquisitive creatures, the horses wanted to check her out and the boldest stepped forward. She kicked him hard on the shin, the crack of her boot resonating loudly. In pain, and with surprise on his gentle face, the horse stepped backward. "That's what I wanted him to do," the woman drawled. "He was in my space and I was teaching him to respect it." The woman went on to demonstrate a lot of things that invaded the horses' space, including whacking one in the mouth, but she didn't see the irony of that. I asked her why she felt the need to be violent towards horses, thus illustrating her shocking disconnection. It appeared to me she feared

> **"**Communication and acquisition of knowledge, of whatever kind, occurs through energy transfer, which horses are constantly alert to.**"**

intimacy with them; was this a mirroring situation, a reflection of deficiency due to what was happening in her personal life? I will never know because she didn't answer.

I find equine shows and demonstrations involving tricks and stunts downright unpleasant because these don't do horses justice. One of the worst illustrations of disconnection I have ever seen was when a rider made his mare lie down during a show so that he could sit and stand on her while she was on the ground. The man announced that this was to illustrate the horse's trust in him. He was so disconnected from the horse that he did not see the haunted look in her eye, that she asked to get up several times, and that to most people watching it was an utterly degrading spectacle, sending a message to the horse, "I am in charge, you are powerless and I can do anything I want with you." I see this type of human domination as a metaphor for trampling on another's feelings. With our family members, friends, and workmates we seek trust, yet we do not expect them to lie down so that we can walk over their bodies to prove it. Why should this be acceptable behavior with horses?

In these cases the horses offered their love and of their best, yet were treated badly in the name of "horsemanship." They were saying, "This is not right. Why don't you get it?" Failing to hear the messages of other beings can open profound wounds, which may take years to heal. Only when we listen to the horse from the heart will a true connection take

---

Broken connection . . .

There are many horses who suffer from a broken connection when they are passed on to new homes. Some take a long time to settle, missing previous friends both human and equine, and, in my experience, an old horse may never fully recover from a move. Special care and patience is needed to help a horse through such times.

. . . and reconnection

It's always gratifying when a horse ends up in a new home that is full of love where needs are fully met. Then we have gone full circle and a connection is formed like a marriage—a commitment and promise to do the right thing through good times and not so good times.

For each of the threads that come together in life and from every angle—the key word is connection.

place, rather than a disconnection. Through paying homage to the ego, any relationship will quickly unravel—whether with humans, who are free to walk away, or horses, who are not, but who nevertheless feel the same bewilderment and betrayal.

Two halves

Because horses read the whole package that we are, the two halves of our inner and outer communication, they are not fooled by actions. I once watched as a psychotherapist bizarrely asked a woman to role-play being a bully towards a horse, so she flapped her arms but initially the animal did not move, instead he snorted and looked confused. Eventually the horse turned and ran, and the psychotherapist then asked the woman to walk towards the horse and touch him. When the horse allowed this to happen we were told it was an example of how forgiving horses are, but it simply demonstrated that the horse knew the woman was acting. The woman went on to say that she had felt very uncomfortable at doing what she had been asked to do, so while waving her arms she had mentally and emotionally said, "I'm so sorry about this. I don't really want you to go away." The horse wondered why a human, yet again, did one thing yet meant another, and forgave that, as horses usually do, conveying a lesson in common sense.

Other people's influences

Our work in building a relationship can be undone by someone's thoughtless actions, which a horse does not like or understand. I see it this way . . . if someone were to attack or hurt us, and a person that we loved and considered a protector stood by and did not stop it, or let the abuser come back again, how would we feel? Disappointed, betrayed, sad? That's how a horse can end up feeling in such situations.

Bracken had become skittish, which I picked up was due to losing faith in his carer, the pony communicating that she had allowed a man to hit him. The woman admitted that the farrier would give the pony a sharp dig in the ribs with the rasp to make him stand still, totally unacceptable behavior on the man's part. When I pointed out to the owner that she would not feel too good about a best friend smilingly standing by while someone thumped her, she was mortified. The relationship had soured not because of what the carer had done, but because of what she had allowed to be done. Fortunately, horses are an example of not holding grudges (although they never do forget) and once the woman realized her error and became protective of the horse, he relaxed in her company.

As sensitive creatures, horses can also become hurt by emotional pain. I once picked up from a horse that he didn't like his carer allowing her friend to laugh at him when he did things wrong in his work. The woman confirmed that this did happen, although she had felt uncomfortable about it. Now, knowing how much it upset the pony, she resolved that she would prevent it from happening again.

On another occasion I observed a rider having a lesson. Around and around she went, until the horse started to swish his tail and flatten his ears. "I think we should stop now, he's had enough," I heard the rider call as she rode past the instructor. "You keep him going until you tell him to stop; it's not up to the horse to dictate how the training goes," she replied. Why should someone else spoil a connection that we strive so hard to make? The horse counsels that we should pay attention when he or she says, "I have had enough. I need to rest because it will be better in the long run for both of us." It's essential to adopt a stance of standing up to others on behalf of the horse.

> **By reflecting what we feel, horses encourage self-reflection.**

The unintentional

With the best will in the world we can get it wrong and often it's our unintentional way of being or lack of foresight that can unsettle a horse.

A vet had asked me to visit a horse with various issues to see what light I could throw on the problem. I was told that this was a very sensitive horse and if he didn't like me, I would not be able to get near him; thankfully, he licked my hands and invited me to touch him. When I asked the horse if anything made him unhappy, he communicated that there was a man he didn't like due to his way of transmitting an unsettling air of tension. It seemed to be the owner's husband, but she told me that he loved the horse dearly and would never do anything harmful. However, she did admit that the horse would not eat in her husband's presence, but considered this to be a quirky trait.

Later the man arrived and out of the corner of my eye I noticed the horse stiffen and step back as he approached. He was a man of few words and I could sense his genuine concern, yet he carried visible signs of stress. Now I knew why the sensitive horse found the man unsettling: he was sending out an unintentional "alarm warning." It had the effect of inducing in the horse the survival instinct of preparing for flight, which was why he stopped eating when the man was close by. The horse was ready to run away from the dominant signal of stress overriding the caring emotions that the man felt deep down.

After explaining the reason for the horse's reaction I went back a couple of weeks later to find the man stroking the horse's neck while he happily munched hay. As always, when we do some work on how we are feeling, and therefore what message we are transmitting, it has a ripple effect with others. People had been commenting on how much more relaxed the man was and that they, too, wanted to share his company rather than shun him. Everyone in the yard said that they were now observing body language in case they could help each other highlight any adverse behavior. Horses are indeed a wonderful prompt for doing some work on self-improvement.

The journey to connection

In order to learn from horses we need to acknowledge that they have something of worth; we may do that consciously or at other times it may come as a flash of inspiration. The journey that we take will have highs and lows, like any trip that we embark on in life. There is no plan or map to follow, and if we focus on an end result, we will miss being fully educated. The learning is in the experience, for in reality there is no destination, only this moment. The most important thing is realizing that the horse is an equal, yet completely different. This is indeed an amazing connection.

4 The quest

We are all seeking something, but what that is will change as we go through life. Connectedness—wanting to be united with all that exists—is a specific feature of people's search for understanding and in this respect horses can help us find what we are looking for. What frequently emerges through interacting with them is a synthesis of the old and the new, our established beliefs and opinions blending with vision and foresight. The process is cathartic and transformational and for many people changes not only their perceptions of horses but of themselves.

Horses carry us home. As well as having a literal meaning, spiritually the horse transports us to a place of sanctuary, a safekeeping for the soul, a route to inner harmony. Over millions of years the horse has evolved to be a unique animal, an embodiment of divine love, which can heal our emotional or mental scars and pain. The valuable lessons taught by horses help our quest to discover the meaning of life and our place in the world. One recurring theme that I come across in my work concerns the wordless signaling by which horses give us honest and ruthless feedback in an uncompromising, explicit way; information that we can readily accept if we are patiently expectant and open to all possibilities. The goodness of others, including equines, so often illuminates our own shortcomings. Because horses are non-judgmental, inviting us to make self-judgments, this allows us to take on board from them what we won't from another source, finding it plausible. If we were to take part in human activities designed to give us feedback about our shortcomings, few of us would be happy with the situation. In fact, we might even accuse the other people involved of off-loading their defects onto us, saying, "It wasn't really me that got it wrong because you were transferring your issues."

By comparison, people are consistently motivated to make changes for the sake of their horse, although it can be very hard to let go of negative behaviors. Also, before we can act decisively and with commitment, we often need lucidity about things going on around us. Once that happens, our focus changes, becoming more coherent as horses challenge us to become better human beings. Because they don't lie or have ulterior motives, horses can help us achieve this. We needn't necessarily be

> **❝**We cannot solve the problems that we have created with the same thinking that created them.**❞**
> *Albert Einstein*

looking for guidance for there are times when we don't think we need it, but horses often spring surprises by infusing people with a new articulation about their lives. It's as if we ask a question along the lines of, "What else is there?" and the horse answers, "Follow me and all will be revealed."

Increasingly, people report to me that being in the presence of a horse makes them feel emotional, such is the intensity of the evolved being they sense, as though a voice is saying: "In this horse guise I am here to help you." This knowledge serves as a reminder of our options, to expand or to flounder, with the horse as a spiritual entity showing us the repercussions of both pathways. Following the way of the horse, we can strive to receive each moment with change or reconciliation; both are part of the flow of life.

Why should horses want to do this for us? I believe that they are part of the growing agreement and campaign by the animal kingdom to save our planet. The horse is the messenger of perception, a reminder of our responsibilities and the link between Father Sky and Mother Earth.

> **❝**An effective leader wants to nurture and does not make a soul feel lost.**❞**

Answers from different sources

The healing horse that we come across may be a horse we care for or we may find a special relationship with a horse that is not ours. It's important to be open beyond our immediate horizons in case we overlook an equine that has something to share with us. Vicky, a vet friend, developed a special rapport with a horse called Wexford, such that he has become a mentor. Whenever she has a bad day, Vicky comes by to hug him. "Of all the horses that I come across I don't know what it is about that guy," she told me, "or what the connection between us is, but I sense his wisdom and strength. It's like when I am with him he infuses me with those qualities, and he heals me."

Sometimes a horse enters a person's life and triggers a life-enhancing shift. Michelle, a teenager living in Australia, was considered to be a loner due to finding the company of animals more relaxing than that of humans. Going through a difficult stage after gaining weight, the girl went to a local riding academy to realize a lifelong ambition of learning to ride, which would also help her to get fitter. One day, a rescued horse arrived in very poor condition and both Michelle and her mother instantly fell in love with him, even though he was not at all nice to them at the time. They saw kindness in his eyes and took him on as their own, calling him Ozzie. A year later both Michelle and the horse were transformed and Michelle finds it very hard to stay away from him, acknowledging, "Looking back at the girl I used to be, I have realized that I am now very different. I have lost weight, made new friends, and stopped closeting myself away in my room."

Michelle had a question for me: "Is what has happened a result of healing shared between myself and my horse? After I met Ozzie everything in my life started to shape and come together." I was able to answer that they had both been transformed by reciprocal healing. Despite his own troubles, the horse had sensed the girl's plight, and she had responded to his generous wisdom. Through the horse's giving nature, the young woman has found a wonderful connection both to him and to herself.

Because they do not know the meaning of the words treachery and betrayal, horses are incapable of standing in front of you pretending to be your friend and then stabbing you in the back. Sometimes I hear people say that a horse is being evil, dishonest, or disingenuous, but it's simply impossible for that to be so. Those are human concepts; horses through their passive nature are the ultimate pacifists.

Wholeness

Horses and humans are, of course, not equal in terms of the material world, yet they are equal in cosmic terms, because everything is part of the whole. The general problem for humans is one of fragmentation, seeing and believing only in separateness where there is actually wholeness. This view of life holds that the universe, the animal kingdom, and ourselves are all separate from one another, creating a division where none exists and in doing so making us lose our way. Fragmentation is reflected in the mind-set that leads to the study of isolated things, not just organisms but even parts of the body, and as such is a reason why so many problems regarding horses are not correctly identified. A fragmented way of thinking also means that humans become less effective at problem solving. Einstein referred to the stance of separation as a kind of optical delusion of consciousness. The human race, because it does not recognize connection and correlation of all that there is, hurtles through history destroying all around it.

The horse, however, educates us to study and embrace the whole of everything, to pull together the scattered parts because wholeness is an unbroken continuum to be treasured—an overview that leads to survival. It means seeing from within as well as being externally aware and, importantly, realizing that fragmentation exists only as a human misunderstanding. Acceptance of wholeness leads to a belief in coopera-

> **Reality**
>
> *Reality is fluid, not fixed, and therefore open to our influence as well as to the horse's influence. Reality is an interaction that changes constantly, depending on input and responses.*

tion rather than competition—exactly how horses teach us to live. The horse can be described as a metaphor for the individual and also for different levels, such as the universe, a problem, a relationship, and so on. Ultimately, the horse is an evolving metaphor for wholeness.

Look at a horse and see that you are part of the same eternity. Freed from the limitations of intellect, you can blend, moving timelessly and effortlessly to synchronize—heartbeats, breath, life itself. Illumination of your worth and potential then follows.

Horse/human interaction

As we go through life looking for inspiration, the quality of relationships can make all the difference to our well-being. When we feel supported, then we are far better able to cope with everyday ups and downs. No two people are the same in the eyes of a horse and we too should view each equine as an individual; what works with one may not with another. Having distinctive mannerisms and being different is not a bad thing in any species, because it is variety that makes the world so interesting. Connection and a happy partnership is not going to happen, however, if we are not suited to a particular horse or a horse is not suited to us— both parties will emulate each other in their dissatisfaction. We will not be all things to all horses and finding the right horse for a partnership that suits us can be elusive. Our perfect horse may be someone else's nightmare and vice versa. If similar problems keep occurring or a particular horse is not "gelling" with us, and we are sure that physical problems/lifestyle are not an issue, it's advisable to do some reflective work. Interaction with a horse can be a confrontation with the "I" that we are, including our actions, intentions, attitude, and agenda.

The influence of personality traits in human/horse partnerships has been noted for many years. Dr. Helen Spence undertook research at Queens University, Belfast, into horse/human correlated behaviors, and the results confirmed just how much people affect the way that horses present themselves. It is a disappointing situation that so many horses are labeled difficult when all that they are doing may be responding to the humans around them. Dr. Spence's work follows on from earlier research, which showed that many riding horses suffered chronic stress as a result of interactions with humans. She concluded that frequently the horse's behavior would match that of a person, and during the research it was noted that horses could change with new carers and attitudes. Possible explanations for similarities between human and horse could be carers projecting personalities onto horses, a horse's personality exerting an influence on carers, a carer's attitudes and personality exerting an influence on the horse, and people selecting horses that in some way resemble them.

Horses also reflect their treatment. In quick succession I was called out several times because the horses that had been acquired for a teenager would "go wrong." Each horse told me the same story about being used incessantly until exhaustion took hold and physical ailments set in. Disappointed, the family would go and buy another and the whole saga would start over again, so I suggested that the boy was not fit to ride until he learned respect. Thankfully he stopped, saving face by telling friends that he was concentrating on exams. With horses, as in all aspects of life, we need to know when we are in over our heads and seek help accordingly, rather than carry on regardless, which is always a recipe for disaster.

When we look for ways to make life better for a horse it helps improve our own life. If a horse is frustrated, we will feel that our world is frustrating. If a horse yearns for freedom, we too become unsettled with relationships. If a horse is being dominated, we attract disruptive people. If a horse is contented, we can be at peace. When we become empowered by listening to our inner wisdom, confidence blossoms.

66 Horses bring us an enigmatic essence of innocence. **99**

Some lessons of transformation

Having sent out a questionnaire to gauge the main areas that inspired people regarding horses, I noticed that in many cases answers were similar or identical, demonstrating that the lessons of horses comprise fundamental truths, although they mean such different things to individuals that their interpretation and benefits are limitless. These are some of the questions and answers.

What do horses teach you?

Patience (70 percent said this); understanding; trust; unconditional love; responsibility; openness; to be truthful; to feel; to listen; to be peaceful;

loyalty; leadership; humility; communication; to be in the moment; not to judge; observation skills; selflessness; to let go; awareness; how to have fun; what's important in life.

How do horses heal you?

They make my heart happy; they are soothing to be with; touching them is healing; by transforming how I am feeling through their affection; through appreciating what I do for them; allowing me to ride and care for them they give me self-confidence; I feel respected in their presence; I enjoy their company; I feel free; because they listen and a lot can be said without words; they bring harmony and balance to my life; they are always there for me knowing how I feel and accepting me for who I am; by helping me see what really matters in life.

What word would you use to describe a horse's gifts?

Forgiveness; non-judgmental; honest; magical; inspiring; compassion; manifold; acceptance; open; loyal; devotion; sensitivity; spiritual; beautiful; loving; truth; wisdom.

What would your life be like without horses?

Empty (most mentioned this); horrible; dull; meaningless; awful; desolate; clouded by the grind of daily life; boring; unbearable; depressing; grey; a void.

Special lessons

"Horses can only teach those who acknowledge the fact that they have something worth teaching, and those who are willing to learn. Even taking a tiny step forward will bring a reward.**"**

In many cases, the same words were used to describe the horse's gifts and how horses healed, reflecting their wholeness. I explore here a few of the concepts that arose during my research.

Freedom

Despite having no knowledge about horses, Valerie could not refuse when offered an aged mare called Amber. The horse was very frail and thin and Valerie felt an instant connection to this old soul, who it seemed still had so much to give. She took Amber to a place where three other elderly horses happily lived and they all became firm friends. Amber blossomed as Valerie tended to her, and grazing the beautiful pastures brought a sheen to the mare's coat.

"From the beginning I had a heart connection to Amber that made no sense to anyone else," Valerie explained. "Even though I had just had my fourth child, with so much to do at home, I needed to be with her. I felt that the mare understood me, having weaned her eighth foal just before I took her on, and I even dreamed about her, such was our instant and deep connection."

Right from the start Valerie could hear Amber talk to her and the message that she could not get out of her mind was: "If you think that you can free me, you are mistaken; but if you know that your freedom is bound to mine, then we can work together."

Carrying her baby in a sling and with the horse on a rope they walked together in the forest, like two old friends, safe in their love for each other. Then Valerie began to get an image of a foal whenever she stood by Amber and the feeling seemed to stem from knowledge in her heart. Everyone said it was impossible, the vet agreeing that at twenty-six the horse was too old to be pregnant. However, Amber got bigger until it became apparent that she was soon to foal. A heightened intensity of awareness developed between woman and horse as they waited for the birth, with Valerie singing to the unborn, such was her powerful love. Amber's colt foal arrived early one morning.

"Amber was so beautiful that day and so strong that I was in awe of her," Valerie remembers. "I kissed the foal on the forehead and said, 'Welcome, Lucero.' Suddenly the births of all my children flashed through my mind and the emotion was overwhelming. There we were, two mothers nursing our last babies in the middle of a field with the sun shining down on us."

The lesson about freedom that had been so prevalent in Valerie's mind began to make sense and her life became enriched in many ways: "This horse has taught me to be strong and proud, to be patient, calm, and unconditional. But most of all, not to lose sight of myself. Thanks to her I have found my courage, inner beauty, and my incredible strength. Amber filled the ache I had had in my heart for years, and which was called many things including postnatal depression. With Amber's help and healing she has set me free and my life is full of passion and love. She has saved me and my family."

The horse teaches that freedom is knowing who you are.

Leadership

At some point, all people involved with horses, whether riding, handling, or taking part in a workshop, will hear the phrase, "You need to be the horse's leader." Often what that actually means is not made clear and methods of control and domination are offered, which can lead to a horse becoming shut down and a person becoming a control freak. If a horse feels threatened, he or she may stop and look at a human, but we have to be careful and not assume, "That horse has accepted me as leader." Instead, we must ask, "What is actually happening?"

I heard a trainer boasting that she had taken an unhandled four-year-old horse from a herd in order to prepare her for sale. It seemed to be of merit that it only took a day using her training program to be able to get a halter on and become the horse's "leader." Probably over the course of the day, the horse became mentally, emotionally, and physically exhausted and, grieving for her friends, by dusk simply gave up. Surely harmony is found through *really* listening to another being, allowing all parties concerned to be equally and fully content with whatever is happening. An effective leader wants to nurture, and does not make a soul feel lost.

Following can be considered more important than the concept of leadership when considering equine behavior. Becoming a horse's leader means inviting the horse to follow, the human guiding the relationship in terms of what needs to be done together, and setting the direction and purpose of interaction. In terms of the spiritual realms, it is the horse that leads the human to discovery and learning, and everyone who has had an association with horses will at some point have been brought down to earth by the realization that if we are not aligned to ourselves, then we will not be effective with them. In the business or political world, people can be hopelessly ineffective and deficient but still be at the top of the tree, because the public may be swayed by all sorts of things that horses have no interest in. In my previous business career I used to daydream during meetings about heralding in horses to show who was being effective and who was not. When a leader exudes an energy with a rich content of authenticity that feels safe to gravitate towards, amazing things can happen, both with people and horses.

In human terms, a leader can be chosen for many different reasons, not least what they look like, their charisma, profile, or verbal persuasion. A human leader may be someone that you don't actually want to follow, who may not have the interests of the group at heart and be self-serving or manipulative; the type of leader who is useless for horses and who does not do much for humanity either. Equines respond to aggression and dominance by avoidance, whereas humans can be attracted to such qualities. If we apply human leadership strategies to horses, without using restraint, force, or fear, then more than likely we will appear insignificant. When we come from a place of congruence they feel comfortable in trusting us. Thus we accomplish becoming an attractive leader, not judged by what is on the outside but what is shining from within. An empowered leader is director of their own thoughts as well as director of their own life.

Horses associate with the other horses that they prefer to be with, remaining close to them, and they may also follow them. In natural herds, the group leader is a mare with an attending stallion, and there are bachelor herds with their own leader. The primary role of the horse leader is to keep the herd safe while at the same time finding places for them to forage and drink. A leader may enter a lesser horse's space, but a lesser horse may never enter the space of a leader without permission. Establishment of the largest space for the leader is common in most social animals. However, a fact largely missed by the horse world is that as social animals horses also establish leadership through space-taking. The horse, like the human, with the biggest space is the leader and we should always respect horses' space because we ask them to respect ours. This awareness will help to awaken our sense of responsibility generally regarding the feelings and needs of others.

Only when calmness prevails and we are in harmony will a horse say from the heart, "I want to be with you and follow your lead."

> **"** Problems are signposts to help us learn. **"**

Patience

Patience can mean sacrificing one's own goals for the benefit of another individual. It also means possessing tolerance, perseverance, and a self-possessed dignity, even in the face of great frustration; manifold attributes that are needed when with horses. When we are impatient and try to cut corners or become angry it will always go wrong for the horse, as well as for us, and for others who may take on him or her. Horses are made to wait for many things in life, often not receiving what they require, silently wondering why humans ignore their requests.

Horses ask us to have patience in knowing them. Lessons are offered methodically, with an invitation to the pupil to consider everything in infinitesimal detail.

Honesty

Horses are truthful; they do not have awareness of how to be any other way. Neither do they fabricate events for gain or make mountains out of molehills. In a world of human perverseness they are a constant in their genuineness and honest with their feedback, which can be hugely comforting because it makes us feel safe. They can, of course, be unpredictable, but that is not dishonesty; it is their programming as prey flight animals.

Horses honestly want to help humans, genuinely enjoying relationships of mutual benefit.

Responsibility

We are wholly responsible for the horses in our care, with a duty to put their needs first. Horses cannot look after themselves when humans take control of their lives. Responsibility also includes selling and breeding, and the future consequences of those lives.

The horse reminds us of our moral accountability to others. Giving the horse our fullest attention is a precious gift.

Respect

Horses challenge us to listen as carefully to them as they do to us. It may take a long time to gain a troubled horse's respect, but in the end each horse is a healer and will want to put that skill to use, depending on our own needs.

The horse has no ego, but instead has a great deal of self-respect.

Trust

Trust means a firm belief in the reliability or truth of an individual. In order to gain trust from a horse we need to be consistently sensitive, patient, and calm. A horse may be accused of not being trustworthy, but that means the people involved have gone wrong in identifying and understanding a problem. A horse that is submissive due to being fearful or dominated is not the same as a trusting horse. Trust is earned through caring behavior and fulfilling obligations of meeting the horse's natural needs. When a horse places his or her confidence in us, we are accepted as a trustworthy friend.

Horses are willing to trust when offered unconditional love. Then the heart of the horse will be light.

Truth

Horses are true to themselves and millions of years of evolution have not corrupted that. They know which people are genuine and which are lacking in consistency. Whether a person's heart is hard as stone or full of love and compassion, the horse identifies this and mirrors that energy back. They invite us to be truthful about the subtleties of our actions, thoughts, and intentions. We are influenced by numerous factors, and for self-healing to take place we must rise to a level beyond whatever caused imbalances.

Horses offer their truth as a healing benefit. The phenomenal perception of the horse is at the heart of their ability to heal.

Movement

Horses are the epitome of movement. There is no more potent way to illustrate movement both physically and spiritually than through the horse, for we can move in directions that previously have been untried or hidden. When sitting on a horse, you can either direct movement or let go and be moved. As well as transporting us across the earth's terrain, horses can move us into exploring an internal landscape where we can embark on a journey of self-discovery. Movement is necessary for change to take place, for when we start moving, we become blessed by experience. Watching the measured movements of the horse, an animal that resists wasting energy, can help to slow us down so that we take on board what's important and where our priorities lie.

In dream analysis, horses often manifest as physical extensions of the dreamer, such as the subconscious desire to move forward in life.

> **"**Man is a being in search of meaning.**"**

Letting go

An emerging science called chronobiology recognizes that all living systems operate in time to the rhythms of life. In tandem with the earth's rotation around the sun and solar geomagnetic conditions, everything, from a fruit fly to a human being, responds to the same twenty-four-hour rhythm. This is not something learned or acquired but a basic property of life. Horses, like all animals, are in tune with cosmic energies and often the solution to a horse's "problem" is to let it be in the natural world.

A rider once asked me to see her competition horse because of his lack of work concentration. When I entered the stable he tried to nudge open the door. Sadness filled me when it closed again and the horse stared up at the roof, ears flicking as he picked up sounds we would never hear. When I learned that the horse had only a couple of hours of free time outside each day I knew that what I could do for him was to tell the owner that a prisoner loses enthusiasm for life. No amount of treats, wall mirrors, nice views, music playing, floral displays, and designer equine clothing will compensate a horse for lack of outdoor herd living.

Inability to let go is born out of insecurity and has a negative effect on relationships; the horse longs to be elsewhere rather than with us, asking, "You're free, why not me too?"

The horse teaches that letting go means that whatever is best for us will be able to find its way home to our heart.

Strength

Horses embody strength in a package of physical, emotional, and spiritual aspects, and also have their own inner strength and resilience. Tuning into our energy states means that the horse senses and absorbs our dysfunctions as well as our spirituality. There are many reasons why we can feel at a low ebb and it can be a sign that we feel powerless about something in our life. We can turn this around by immersing in the vitality and strength of a horse. Absorbing his or her inherent goodness can shift our attention away from everyday concerns.

For eight years Judy had suffered from chronic fatigue, having woken up one morning to find herself too weak to get out of bed. Eventually she started to recover, and although Judy's family was very supportive, she felt that something was missing from her life. An enlightened doctor encouraged Judy to get back into horses as he felt that this could help her regain her full health. Judy told me that this was exactly what had happened to her, saying, "I then found Scrumpy, a very loving pony. I sensed that he was looking for someone to love him in return. By coming together we have both become complete. Through this connection I have become strong again."

The horse can empower us and revitalize our energy.

Belief

Choosing to believe in oneself and concentrating on positive aspects can make a big difference to self-esteem and this, in turn, enhances in us energy that horses are drawn to. Horses believe in themselves and problems occur when we push them unnaturally and they either do not want to, or cannot, do what we ask of them.

By confidently listening to their needs and setting our own agendas aside, we take a step nearer to knowing horses, and through them other beings too.

Sharing

In my survey, the resounding reply to the question "What would life be like without horses?" was "empty." Horses are a comforting and supportive influence the world over. *They have offered to be our guides because they love us unconditionally.*

People often feel profound love, yet have not learned how to express it. Horses, by being loving, allow this to happen. Horses also teach that we can't make anyone love us; all we can do is allow ourselves to be loved.

One benefit of being with horses is that they can help people feel good about themselves, and this in turn helps how they relate to others. Horses offer us the opportunity to shine from within. We become able to recognize the beautiful qualities in others when we have a good inner template.

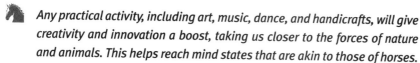

Get creative

Spending time with horses can bring us to discover our hidden talents, leading to personal development. To enable this to take place more easily, it's beneficial to explore creativity to increase sensitivity to this process. Humans often get caught up in things that are structured but this doesn't necessarily keep us safe; rather, it closes us in and prevents our creativity from surfacing.

Any practical activity, including art, music, dance, and handicrafts, will give creativity and innovation a boost, taking us closer to the forces of nature and animals. This helps reach mind states that are akin to those of horses.

Encourage the flow of natural thoughts. Spending a few minutes a day writing down whatever comes into your mind is a good way to tap into inner thoughts and an idea related to a horse may develop. Sitting quietly and letting the imagination roam unchecked helps remove the clutter of everyday life. By developing this technique, you can use it to tune into many areas of life.

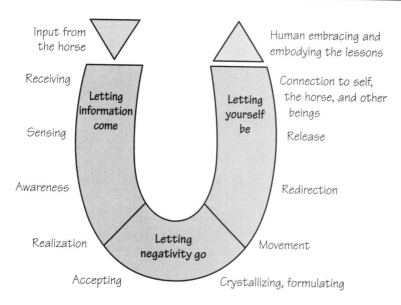

Stages of awareness through being with horses

5 Power to move between worlds

Learning how to be oneself is challenging and it is through experience that we accomplish this. We all have the inner resources that we need to maneuver our way through the world, but to help us in this the horse entices us into a moment where our intuition and instincts are inseparably linked. Self-awareness follows. The horse is fundamental in helping us realize that congruence with the universe is the ultimate education. "Let's get back to basics" could be a saying invented by horses, reminding us that we are part of the indivisible whole.

Horses are unequaled in their influence on us, representing a link between our outer and inner worlds, relating intelligence in abundance and often profoundly redirecting us out of the wilderness. The resolution to a problem may not be apparent in our everyday world but be lurking on a deeper level; a recess that we have yet to uncover. Although we talk about our world, or the horse's world, it's actually not that simple, for everything is part of the world. Another way to look at it is to think of compartments that cannot truly be separated, for each affects the other. Spending time with a horse means experiencing his or her "world compartment." Because horses do not have a concept of energetic segregation, they offer us the opportunity to understand how to blend with the whole. This skill is actually already within us, but for some reason it is now mainly dormant in many of us, until activated by the connection with horses.

While humankind is distracted from nature, the horse is not, being motivated by the vitality and resonance of universal energy fields. We share the same planet yet move in different worlds, seeing things from a different perspective and attuned to different priorities. By understanding how horses perceive us, and learning about the nuances of spirituality, we can unlock our inner talents to explore intimate encounters within the realm of the horse. Parallel worlds are always overlapping and blending, but somehow humankind has, on the whole, lost the skill of tuning into the world of the universal intelligence and consciousness. Horses and other animals have not lost this ability and constantly bridge worlds; it is impossible for them to switch this off. We can, however, all easily regain this aptitude to help realize our dreams.

> **"**We must never doubt the power within for that is where change is instigated.**"**

Inner worlds and relationships

An ex-banker in his mid-forties, Alasdair's only previous experience of horses had been sitting on one when he was five years old. Now, as he stood in the middle of an arena while two horses were brought in, his first thought was how big they were. Naturally Alasdair felt nervous, and even very experienced horse people will admit to feeling particularly alert when around strange horses.

Both of the horses that day were feeling full of the joys of spring and they spent a while cantering around, bucking, leaping, rolling in the sand, and generally playing, as the class observed how horses react at liberty. When the horses were ready they came to investigate and make contact—a very special experience for this mostly non-horsey group.

The horses moved off again and Alasdair was asked to make contact by moving among them, before seeing if he could encourage them to follow him for a while. The coach asked Alasdair to walk purposefully towards the horses but I noticed he looked like a man pretending to walk purposefully rather than feeling it—a big difference. The energy around him and the horses was discordant and they therefore turned their backs to Alasdair, not in a threatening way, but disinterestedly. They wandered around whenever he stood near them and generally there was an air of fragmentation. Alasdair went back to his colleagues looking unhappy; things were not working out. This man, who had led teams of people at a high level in business, could not make a horse show him any interest and the look on his face was one of consternation and disenchantment.

One of the workshop leaders stepped forward and took Alasdair aside to have a chat, and after a couple of minutes he walked across the arena to where the horses had gathered. Something had changed; there was a different atmosphere around Alasdair and a palpable aura of healing energy radiated between him and the horses, which all of us watching commented on. This time the horses didn't move off but watched the man intently as he approached them. Alasdair held out his hands palm upward, then touched the horses, stroking and patting them on the neck, before turning back towards the rest of the class. Incredibly, both of the horses followed, wanting to join him now wherever he was going, moving along a few paces behind him. This sign of trust would have been an achievement for an experienced horse person, let alone someone who had only spent around an hour in their company.

I was intrigued; what, I wondered, had been said to Alasdair that had made such a difference, resulting in the bonding? Four key words had enabled this to happen: "Connect with the horses."

"I suddenly realized," said Alasdair, "that I hadn't done that. So I said to the horses via my mind, '*Let's do this*'—by offering an intent I thereby created a wanting to connect. I projected a warmth towards the horses like I would to my children and then it all came together, because I saw the horses watching me and I knew that they were listening. The difference in the horses' response to me was quite dramatic."

Alasdair had begun to realize how much power our inner world has on influencing relationships and the benefits of this when harnessed. People are sensitive to the energies of others, but unlike the horse we often don't realize what is happening. When we commit to awareness, symbiotic relationships follow, leading to each individual in the team being able to operate on a more productive level.

I asked Alasdair what he had learned from the horses' responses that day. He thought for a moment and then said: "Being with the horse is about creating a feeling space, not a thinking space. It has been a revelation—I never knew that horses were so intuitive; it's been a very powerful awakening for me that the horses heard my silent communication. The horses have taught me today not to be afraid to open up and to communicate naturally rather than how other people expect me to."

This lesson is something we can all take into our everyday lives, including the workplace and social interactions. For positive things to happen in any association, we need a connection to take place, and we make that through the projection of emotion—not just by thinking about it. All the time that Alasdair tried to think his way into the horses' world, they were having none of it. As soon as he projected love, his world became synergistic with that of the horse, revealing a bridge that he could readily access and traverse. It was a two-way journey: not only could the wisdom and the healing of the horse be received, he could send out more of the same.

> " Through their connectedness to ancient rhythms horses show us a place they have never forgotten. When we remember where we come from, everything changes and triumphantly we can behold our beauty. "

Reaching out

As long as humankind has been on earth animals have been part of their world. As hunter-gatherers we have encoded in our genetic makeup information about observing animals and our ancestors learned how to interpret their messages in the knowledge that animal behavior can indicate danger. Horses still look out for our safety in terms of our emotional well-being as they signal when something within our internal landscape is going awry.

Bridging the world between our attitudes with the subliminal power of the horse can often take place just by observation of the horse's healing powers. Joan and her colleagues were on a team-building day and she was hiding some very bad news; that morning her doctor had left a text message on her phone to say she needed to call urgently to discuss some test results. She knew that this could only mean her breast cancer was active again, raising the specter of facing her mortality.

Instinctively, Joan felt that she wanted to take her burden to one of the horses, a small bay thoroughbred that she felt drawn to. Her colleagues watched as Joan went over to the horse, which immediately curled his neck around her, resting his chin very gently onto her back—it was the nearest that you could get to a horse hug. Woman and horse stayed like that for quite a while; the horse offering whatever was needed and the woman soaking it up. When Joan moved away, the horse followed like an anxious parent checking that a child is safe. She didn't want to discuss with her colleagues what she had felt, other than to say that she had been given fortitude to deal with what was to come. Strength, of course, the horse has in abundance, not least spiritual.

It was noticeable that the other people in the group had also been greatly affected by watching the healing horse in action. They were subdued and thoughtful and a marked change took place with one man in particular. Normally considered crass and thoughtless, he started to display uncharacteristic consideration and caring towards the others. The most amazing thing had happened that day; the horse reached out and touched not just the heart and soul of the troubled woman but those watching, who also chose to open up to what was offered. We just have to be accepting as the horse reaches out, homing in on where we need help, which may be in an emotional, mental, or physical sense. Like hands joining, our worlds combine and in that space and stillness the horse invites us to progress and to heal.

> **"**People frequently report that they look at all animals in a different way through their interaction with horses. They have a greater respect and understanding of their role in the world.**"**

Your world

Your world is your own even though it blends and overlaps with the world of others, and horses have an uncanny knack of being able to target specific areas in it. Out and about one day, I felt myself drawn to enter a small shop where I became involved in a conversation with an assistant about horses. The woman poured her heart out concerning her daughter who was going to university and sending her pony to a friend, but the donkey companion who she felt bonded to would have to go elsewhere. Emotion welled up as she spoke and tellingly said, "In my heart I feel this is the wrong thing to do, but I have no equine experience and the experts tell me I should let them go."

With insight I ventured, "This is about your need, isn't it?" The woman told me she did indeed have a strong feeling of wanting to care for these loving and demonstrative animals, and it would fill a void in view of the fact that her daughter was going away for three years. Her own dream as a child had been to have a pony and through her daughter she had been able to glimpse the world of equines. However, she felt selfish in wanting to keep the pony and donkey, having all her life given to others.

I explained that the person she was depriving this time was herself. It was a multifactorial lesson; those animals needed her as much as she needed them, and they were teaching her to think of her own needs for a change, a very valid point. They had only just begun the process of learning from each other, with much more to come. Empowered, she stood her ground, allowing herself fulfillment and her world to be enriched.

As individuals we all move within our own world, and we may also belong to a group world. There are worlds within worlds, each with a physical, spiritual, and metaphorical element attached to it. Horses as multicultural teachers have something to offer, no matter who we are, where we live, or what part of society we belong to.

> **"**The horse is a powerful messenger and guide, teaching connection with ourselves and with the world around us.**"**

An open world

One of the horse's gifts is to open our world to meeting others in order for reciprocal healing to take place. Through horses I have made a multitude of friends from around the world, some of whom I only know through correspondence, but all the people that I come into contact with have added to my knowledge and awareness. It's encouraging to know that the world is full of people who love and honor horses, doing their best to help them as much as they are helped by them. Contact with a horse can bring together all the pieces of the jigsaw puzzle so that everything falls into place, and every day someone's world changes because of this, as Joanne's story illustrates. Joanne bought a terrified and badly treated filly, not realizing at the time that she would be presented with an aspect of happiness not previously experienced. She explained:

Dolci is, without a doubt, my soul mate and I couldn't imagine life without her. I believe that everything happens for a reason and I know that I was supposed to meet Dolci on the day that I did, and that she was going to make my life much happier. She had a look in her eye that said, "Take me with you." Now, every day she makes me laugh and we talk the whole time we are together . . . I really can't find the words to explain how much I feel for her. She is the love of my life and I am never letting her go.

Looking in the wrong place

Sometimes humans and horses are poles apart because the human is looking in the wrong place for information. A workshop leader once surprised me by saying that he had watched classes where nothing was taking place, and that he always set up exercises for his clients so that things could happen. I can only assume that he never spends time watching horses. There is always something going on, not least that the horse susses us out and our own senses are listening to energy fields unraveling and responding. When something is made to happen, the subtleties of a lesson are lost and what we really need to know will pass us by. Through ignoring the natural and seeking to control the world, and worlds within worlds, we lose our way. The price is spiritual emptiness and thus the individual becomes trapped.

Asking a question

When we are asleep, the body rests while a world of inner activity takes place as the subconscious sifts through and analyzes all the information that we have been absorbing at quantum level. A useful exercise is to ask before going to sleep, "What is my horse trying to teach me and how should I interpret that?"

In the morning an insight will have come to the foreground of your consciousness. It may be one word, a sentence, an image, or a feeling and sometimes may not make much sense. Hang onto whatever comes—at some point during the next day or so you will begin to unravel the mystery with the horse's help.

Becoming grounded

Standing barefoot on the earth for fifteen minutes a day can get us "grounded." At any time in life, when we need to improve our vitality, mentally or physically, this is a very helpful thing to do.

Free electrons from the earth are nature's own antioxidants and most humans have become electron-deprived by not enough contact with the earth. Electrons travel into organisms and the higher that we get from the ground, such as in tall buildings, the further away we become from the natural antioxidants needed for our optimum health. This fact has been made use of by some professional cyclists who use earth-grounding techniques to help improve performance; as a result, they experience increased stamina and faster injury repair.

Shoes with synthetic soles prevent us from receiving the essential electrons that we need, whereas animals are directly connected to the earth (provided they spend time outdoors). Metal horseshoes are good conductors of electrons, unlike synthetic ones. The more that we get in touch with natural forces, the easier it is for us to connect to horses by operating through transference of energy.

Scientists conducting animal studies have found another benefit in the earth—a "friendly" bacteria, mycobacterium vaccae, which they claim has the same uplifting effect as antidepressant drugs. Researchers at Bristol University and University College London found that the bacteria stimulated the immune system, activating neurons in the brain, which produce the mood-enhancing chemical seratonin, the deficiency of which has been linked to depression. The studies helped scientists understand how the body communicates with the brain and why a healthy immune system is important for maintaining mental health.

Horses love to roll in the dirt and apart from the enjoyment and physical relaxation that it brings, I believe that they also benefit from the absorption of free radicals and beneficial bacteria. Blocks that we place preventing horses from acting according to their innate wisdom will dilute our connection with them and distance us from earth harmony.

I have seen people from every discipline upset horses through their disruptive energy, which they were obviously unaware of. This is one reason why, before I go near a horse, I take time to become centered and grounded, either by standing barefoot for a few minutes or doing a short meditation.

> **"** Being open is valuing every form of life as precious, thereby a connection forms rebounding around the world and touching all life. **"**

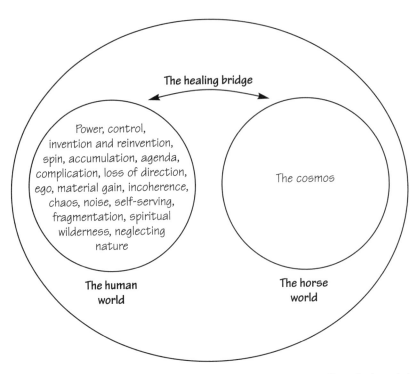

Worlds within worlds: above and beyond everything that may happen in our lives, the horse helps us become liberated so that we can feel the thread of connection to the rest of the universe. The horse offers security in that no matter how much our material world may change, the world of healing that we can be transported to is a constant to return to whenever needed. By their reflective contribution horses suffuse our everyday world with a reminder that indeed there is a holier dimension. When and if we allow them to, horses lead us out of a place of sameness into a world of possibility. Horses surround us with their all-embracing philosophy infiltrating hearts and minds. "Just be."

The enduring quality of the horse is that he or she carries the positive aspects of human nature without the self-destructive habits, which collectively become world-destructive. This is why, I believe, so many people gravitate towards the spiritual safety of the healing horse.

The power of being positive

It helps horses if we are harmonized and filled with positive energy, not least because this makes them feel safer and more secure in our presence. When we are charged with positive energy, it's much easier to become attuned to others and thus sense what we need to do to help. We can do the following exercise when we want to enhance a relationship, or if the horse is injured, ill, or upset about something. It's also a useful exercise before handling or riding if experiencing difficulties. In fine weather I like to do this exercise outside.

Stand with feet slightly apart, hands by your side with palms against your thighs. With eyes closed, breathe slowly and deeply.

Visualize white light pouring down onto your head, surrounding your whole body and onto the ground around your feet.

Make the light shimmer so that you radiate luminescence and anyone looking at you would be dazzled.

Now absorb this light so that a limitless stream circulates within your whole body.

Take a deep breath, open your eyes, and invite a feeling of the warmth and love for all life to flow through you and outwards.

Now go and see your horse and let him or her share your positive energy.

Our cure

An incredible fact about horses is that their teaching is very simple: be genuinely kind and honest and act from your heart. The interpretation, application, and permutations of this lesson are endless.

We may say that a horse "saves us"; however, he or she is a signpost to a journey that proves to be beneficial for us to take. Thus we learn a way of interpreting what someone else is doing in response to our behavior, and how that impacts on our life.

The horse is not the cure for our problems, but brings about a cure within us.

6 The heart of the matter: thinking and feeling

"How can I help you?" is the perfect way to open a dialogue with a horse. "How can I help you?" the horse offers in return. Generosity of spirit is what makes meeting the horse such a potent encounter, and once we open our hearts and minds there are endless opportunities for mutual healing to take place. The most significant things we can learn from horses cannot be seen, smelled, touched, or questioned by the mind, but are felt in the heart. At the heart of a horse's ability to help is an incredible perception.

As well as responding to his own kind, the horse's mind is bombarded by a stream of nuance from the human brain, long before it filters through to become our body language or verbal commands. Due to the horse's uncanny ability to read our subconscious—at a level at which the mind is not fully conscious, but nevertheless influences our actions—they are aware of resulting subtle and dynamic energy shifts. This often leads us to ponder, "Why did my horse do that?" Before we are even consciously aware of a thought and have narrowed our focus to generate an action, our ideas have been formulated at a creative and intuitive level, and it is this early stage that horses seem to be aware of. The horse's intuitive radar constantly picks up on our internal chatter. Of course, it's impossible for us not to be thinking at any given time, but we can control what we think in order to improve our communications.

Consciousness can be either coherent or incoherent. Each of us has an individual consciousness that shapes our identity, and groups have a collective consciousness. Our individual consciousness influences the whole—the energetic state of all beings—just as the whole influences us in a symbiotic energy exchange. This is true for all forms of life, each species influencing and interacting with all that there is. When around horses I have learned to present as best as I possibly can a "neutral zone" whereby I focus only on linking to the horse via interspecies energy vibrations and avoid letting my mind wander off target.

Likewise, with handling and riding, concentration helps us form a dynamic rapport. When things go wrong, a useful question to ask is:

"Have I become too conscious of myself and forgotten the horse?" By asking this we improve our awareness, raising the bar. The enhanced interplay may possibly result in our being more successful in competitions, but only if the horse is capable of doing what we want. If someone asked me to run a mile I could not, no matter how much that person tuned into me! Horses are similar to us, with varying sizes, ages, shapes, types, personalities, and abilities, and they ask us to take the individual needs of each into consideration, to see what is possible.

People are often attracted to horses because they want to master riding them—the oneness of sharing that power and spirit, which many moons ago was my own initial motivation. It is not an easy skill to achieve because very quickly the complications of one thinking mind interacting with another sets in, including the fact that horses have their own intentions and desires, which may conflict with ours. Being a willing partner, the horse may allow himself to be overruled, but not always, depending how much of the conscious state is influenced by instincts.

66 ... and I whispered to the horse: 'trust no man in whose eyes you do not see yourself reflected as an equal. 99
Don Vincenzo Giobbe, c.1700

Non-human animal intelligence

People with a heightened sense of awareness naturally know that species other than humans have a world of their own intellect. Other animals are not just robotically programmed to go through life on a level of eating and procreating. There is too much hard evidence pointing to a complexity and intelligence in non-human animals—rendering human superiority an unsustainable theory.

When I read in the media about scientists "discovering" amazing sentience in a group of animals, to me it is just scratching the surface of the blindingly obvious. For example, chimpanzees have been found to make complex tools to hunt with and even to plan for the future. In 2002, a crow called Betty made the news when *Science* magazine reported that she was able to fashion complicated hooks out of pieces of wire to retrieve food from a tube—even chimps cannot do this. Parrots are also thought to actually understand elements of human speech, while other birds have been observed playing tricks on each other, including hiding food. These facts are just the tip of the iceberg. If humankind bothered to spend more time observing the other nations that comprise non-human species, it would be universally realized just how sophisticated their worlds are.

In the book *Animal Architects*, James L. Gould and Carol Grant Gould offer overwhelming evidence that intelligence is not only a human attribute or absolute; rather, it exists in all life-forms in tiers of mental ability. We are not going to learn very much of worth from horses until we realize and accept that they are included with us in the echelons of intelligence and must be allowed freedom of expression for this to manifest. Horses are physically extremely powerful, but not dexterous like other animals. Due to the way that they are put together, horses will never be able to make a hook out of a piece of wire with their feet and go fishing, but I believe that one day there will be a global scientific eureka moment acknowledging that horses have a phenomenal emotional intelligence and even a psychic one.

I further maintain that there will also come a time when everyone will recognize the existence of a stream of energetic intelligence through which all life communicates. In my experience, the universal intelligence is elusive if approached with just the analytical left brain, but very easy to access through activating the creative right brain, not to mention the heart. The heart is not just an organ but a center of energy and it is also a "mind." By reaching our heart center, the horse teaches us to participate with others in ways that the intellect alone does not understand.

Emotional intelligence

Intelligence is not just about learning or remembering something. We all have an innate emotional intelligence, a self-awareness, which links with universal intelligence. Proximity with the horse seems to help people develop their emotional intelligence, thereby discovering at their core a calmness that radiates outwards and can be felt by surrounding people. This process appears to be ongoing—it seems that we can "top up" our emotional intelligence by regular association with horses. All of our emotions can teach us something and the horse can help us become emotionally balanced. Entering a serene state may take great effort, depending where we are at in life, but when practiced a few times it becomes easier to key into. The horse is resigned and will wait for us to work it out, no matter how long we take.

A keystone of emotional intelligence is being aware of feelings as they occur but not being swept away by them. By reading our feelings, horses must also experience them; therefore, we need to be aware of how much they take on board, which can lead to their depletion and even illness. Through living a natural lifestyle, the members of a herd can heal each other.

> **"**All that holds us back is what we think—and what we think we can't do.**"**

79

Something is going on

Evidence obtained from over twenty studies using magnetic resonance imaging (MRI) suggests that brain-to-brain communication can occur. Orthodox neuroscientists maintain that such communication is impossible because brains depend solely upon their sensory systems for incoming information. These studies indicate otherwise, however, so something else must be taking place—a transfer of energies unseen to the human eye yet producing measurable effects.

In another set of experiments, human neurons from a common stock were divided into two batches. After the electrical activity of the neurons was measured, one culture was shielded by layers of foil. The other was exposed to pulses from a low-level laser and scientists were surprised to find the neurons in the other culture generating simultaneous readings in synchronicity. Despite being separated and isolated, the two cultures shared some form of communication; there was an intelligence connecting them. This evidence and other pieces of research increasingly suggest a universal intelligence uniting all life, running through everything right down to quantum level. (A quantum is a basic unit of matter or energy, from 10,000,000 to 100,000,000 times smaller than the smallest atom.) No one actually knows where a cell ends and the rest of the world begins. This helps us to understand that horses are more connected to us, and we to them, than we may have previously considered.

> " The brain gives the heart its sight. The heart gives the brain its vision. " *Kall*

The heart and mind connection

Cellular memory is the idea that cells contain information about personalities, histories, and individuality. The discovery of cellular memory has led some researchers to conclude that when an organ is placed in a recipient, the energy and information stored in the organ may be passed on to the recipient, in particular in the case of heart transplant patients.

Through my own work I know that cells have memories because I can scan the body of a horse and pick up information, both physical and emotional, residing in certain areas, and have long believed in a superior form of heart intelligence. This is confirmed by Professor Candace Pert, a biochemist who maintains that every cell in the body has its own "mind" and she has discovered that the heart and the body send messages to each other through chains of amino acids, previously thought to exist only in the brain. Scientists at the Institute of HeartMath in the U.S. have discovered neurons—brain cells of the type shown to have memory—in the heart.

Further research has shown that communication between heart and brain is an ongoing dynamic and two-way dialogue. These scientists have also discovered that when people hold hands, one person's heartbeat can be measured in the other's brain waves. In some cases, even though only one person in the pair was in a loving or appreciative state

Aspects of energy

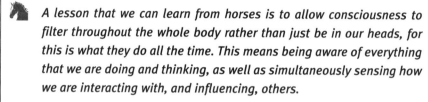 A lesson that we can learn from horses is to allow consciousness to filter throughout the whole body rather than just be in our heads, for this is what they do all the time. This means being aware of everything that we are doing and thinking, as well as simultaneously sensing how we are interacting with, and influencing, others.

Consciousness is about "being," not "becoming"—which is a state of change or evolution.

The emotional state affects the way that both humans and horses perceive and react to the world. It's important to always be aware that our thoughts influence the emotional level of horses.

Our emotions and thoughts are energy footprints, on which the horse will focus.

Heart rhythms become disorganized when experiencing negative thoughts and emotions, while emotions such as love, compassion, and empathy are associated with orderly patterns. Horses sense what is in our hearts and our emotions become instructions telling them how to act when in our presence.

Being in a loving or appreciative state means that our heart energy can become in synch with that of the receiver. If we feel loving towards a horse, then he or she will reciprocate, transmitting healing energy.

Our intellectual and logical aspects can cause us to lose connection with the horse, by taking over from, and swamping, the heart intelligence. When there is balance between the heart and the mind, we can become deeply connected to the awesome potential offered us by the horse.

81

at the outset of the experiment, the heart rhythms of both nevertheless became coherent. This gives us a clue as to just how close we can become to horses through touch and our thoughts. A horse's resting heart rate is slower than a human's so perhaps the reason why we so often feel calm after spending time with them is due to coherence with their heart rhythm. Scientists call this coherence of energies "entraining."

There is a danger in becoming too brain-focused when looking at horse/human relationships and we need to be more aware of the heart's intelligence. We can open up to this through patience, humility, being gentle, and sending thoughts of love to all other living beings. The brain mind does not organize received information very well; however, the heart mind does—one reason why it's important to listen to our heart as well as our head. The heart leads the connection and the heart mind gives us the wherewithal to understand what it is about, through our feelings and emotions. This then triggers something in the brain leading to rationalization and understanding.

We cannot make headway with horses just by being analytical—yes, we must understand the fundamental nature of horses, but in tandem we need to invite our soul to meet their spirit. The heart is the connector in this process and is an influential messenger.

On my desk is a much-treasured letter sent to me many years ago by a twelve-year-old girl called Emily, which she signs off with: "Keep listening with your heart, not just your ears," because, she explains, horses gave her that advice to pass on to others.

> **"** And of course the brain is not responsible for any of the sensations at all. The correct view is that the seat and the source of sensation is the region of the heart. **"**
> *Aristotle*

Touching hearts

We have been brainwashed by conventional scientists into thinking that intelligence lies purely in the brain. With all the amazing healing experiences that I have had with horses, I have felt a tightening of my chest area as they occurred, a realization that I am connecting heart to heart with the horse, from where deep communication stems. People frequently tell me about sensations in their upper body when with horses. Sometimes this is accompanied with feelings of the deepest love, but always with enhanced knowledge. This sort of experience can, and does, happen to anybody and at any time.

Nikki's horse Whiz came into her life after Nikki had gone through a period of being bullied at school. Whiz and Nikki needed each other and became best friends. One evening, Nikki was drawn to look proudly at a picture of Whiz and felt strongly compelled to send her love. Then, staring at the photo, Nikki sent a message to the horse that she would always be there for her. Suddenly Nikki had the sensation of her heart feeling full; her chest then became very tight, before she was overwhelmed with emotion. In that moment, Nikki heard a message from Whiz saying that she loved her too, very much, and that everything was OK. This made Nikki burst into tears, yet at the same time there was a feeling of great comfort. Because of this mystical exchange, the relationship moved onto a deeper level resulting in Nikki understanding the horse better.

Danny also had a heart experience, but of a different kind. It was a beautiful day as the boy sat by the little Shetland pony, chatting away to her. I came across Danny doing this during a trip to a horse rescue center that a group of autistic children had been visiting for a few weeks and this was their last day. The pony mare stood patiently while Danny talked about anything and everything; about his day, about what they had been doing, and how much he liked her. Kneeling down, I asked the boy if the pony could speak to him. "Of course," he said. "They all speak to us." And he waved a hand in the direction of a paddock where some ex-racehorses grazed.

"How do you know that they talk to you, Danny?" I asked.

"Here," he answered, tapping his chest with a hand curled into a ball. "I feel it here."

"What is that place where you feel the horses and ponies speak to you?"

"It's my heart," the boy replied.

It was a humbling experience for here was a boy considered to have severe learning difficulties, yet he could naturally pick up the invisible energies through which equines communicate. He would never understand an explanation of how or why that was so, of scientific studies or quantum physics. It didn't seem to matter that his cognitive skills were not functioning fully; Danny could resonate with horses on their wavelength. It was quite amazing and he would not know or appreciate that there are people who spend a lifetime with horses who do not make that deep connection with them. The boy's time with the horses had allowed him to investigate more than how to groom and feed them. Danny knew that the horses spoke from their hearts to his and this phenomenon was totally natural to him. He didn't need to think about it or analyze it, and that is a truly wonderful gift because it presents opportunities for understanding significant and fundamental truths about existence.

> " Horses can get right inside our heads and hearts, a connection that has endless possibilities. "

83

Thinking like a horse

Humans and horses have more or less the same brain parts, but in different proportions, giving us clues to how they may think and feel. The three main parts in the mammalian brain are the cerebellum, cortex, and limbic system.

- **The cerebellum** deals with mobility, balance, and muscle tone and is much larger in the horse, a flight animal that is a master of movement. Foals can walk, trot, and canter within hours of birth, a sign of their superior natural physical intelligence.

- **The cortex** is involved with cognitive processes, such as learning, analysis, self-awareness, communicating, and consciousness. This part of the brain is bigger in humans and we are good at studying, invention, writing, reading, making things, and using verbal language. The visual cortex is responsible for processing thoughts and cannot distinguish between a real image and an imagined one. In fact, during a study by David Spiegel at Stanford University, mental instructions were shown to be more important than visual images—the mind-over-matter concept.

- **The limbic system** has to do with body-brain links, reproduction, temperature regulation, feelings, and emotions and is a similar size in humans and horses. We can therefore assume that horses have a similar capacity to feel emotions as strongly as we do. The fact that we are more complex due to our thinking and analytical faculties can lead us to experience both difficulties and successes, and because we are so complicated it's a lifelong endeavour to understand just what we are all about. Thinking like a horse when in the company of one can help us in this matter because it's a liberating process, grounding us in the present and freeing us from becoming misguided or having disoriented thoughts.

66 We are limited only by the limitations of our mind. **99**

The brain does not differentiate between a thought and an action; indeed, the thought of an action creates the same pattern in neurotransmission as the action itself. The brain sends instructions to muscles whether we think about carrying out an action or we actually perform it. Therefore, to return to the subject outlined at the start of this chapter, the first lesson of handling or riding horses should be that: "Thoughts produce the same mental instructions as action. Just the thought is enough to produce the neural instructions to carry out the physical act." Horses are a very good barometer of this process taking place. Because horses respond to our desire for change, we need to become aware of what we are thinking, otherwise the relationship that we are trying to build up can go haywire. Horses also naturally preserve physical energy as tension uses up vitality, which may be needed for flight. By learning to do the same through self-restraint we can avoid the muscular overload that leads to fatigue.

Fully engaging

Through the horse we have a wonderful opportunity to reach into a deep and powerful exploration of our psyche. Many scientists now concur that it is through quantum frequencies that the brain sends messages via a complex programming system. In other words, the brain has been discovered to interact through the unseen realms of energy—not a surprising "discovery" to those who have already taken the step to raise their consciousness to the level at which animals communicate.

> **"The best way to relate to a horse is with courage to follow our heart."**

Evidence compiled by Richard Davidson, a neuroscientist and psychologist at the University of Wisconsin's Laboratory for Affective Neurosciences, has shown that the "hard wired" brain theory is outdated. This is the concept that brain functions are fixed in certain locations. Instead it appears that the brain can revise itself throughout our life, depending on the nature of our thoughts; incredibly, consciousness seems to form the brain.

During concentrated periods of focus there is integration between the right and left hemispheres of the brain in a particularly harmonious manner; indeed, the evidence demonstrates that the brain works best when operating in totality. The old belief that the halves of the brain always operate more or less independently is therefore thrown into question. When in a state of stress, however, we do use predominantly one hemisphere of the brain, either the right or left side. Using the left brain means that we apply analytical powers, whereas using the right brain means that we employ intuitive faculties. Everyone is either predominantly left- or right-brained under stress and because of this, we become less capable of problem-solving in a crisis. If our response to stress is mostly right-brained, it means we are more likely to want to escape. Of course, the horse will sense this in us, inducing the desire to run away as well. Therefore, in any stressful situation it is best to stay focused and calm, allowing both hemispheres to be balanced and integrated, applying a whole-brain creativity to problem-solving. It's a reason why instructors encourage horse people to "fully engage."

Through our fears and stress triggers, we can play or replay mental images and these are never hidden from equines. The energy of such images will be picked up by other people, too, who although they may feel unsettled around us will not, unlike a horse, know why. Emma asked me to see if I could help with Micki, a pony with severe skin problems who could be dangerous in traffic. Micki conveyed to me that Emma was, in fact, the nervous one. It drove him crazy when she rode him, constantly presenting him with images of cars crashing into them, so when a vehicle approached, he became distraught. If I was out with someone who kept shouting, "We're going to have an accident," then I too would want to part from their company. The horse was also picking up on the fact that Emma was not happy in her job and her constant anxiety was making him tense, hence his aggravated skin problems. A review of Emma's frame of mind resulted in dramatic relationship improvements with Micki and taught her generally to take on new ventures without expecting them to fail.

> 66 He makes my heart smile. 99
> *Jane, about her horse Turbo*

Horses teach us about their skill of being in the moment and having presence of mind. When we are disconnected from this we experience separation. Instead, from the horse we learn that presence of mind reconnects and anchors us with our inner power, enabling us to become aware of thoughts, feelings, and surroundings. Through this we can avoid replaying what's been or contemplating what is to come.

The Power of Now becomes One World

Heartwarming

This is an exercise that I have devised to help people connect on the deepest level with equines.

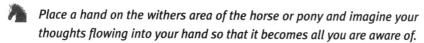 *Place a hand on the withers area of the horse or pony and imagine your thoughts flowing into your hand so that it becomes all you are aware of.*

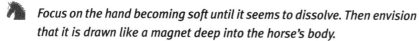 *Focus on the hand becoming soft until it seems to dissolve. Then envision that it is drawn like a magnet deep into the horse's body.*

Now open yourself up so completely that you sense a hand reaching out to meet yours from within the horse. This hand will arise and unfold, touching your fingertips like a kiss before nestling in the palm of your hand. When this happens, hold the hand gently for it is the energy of your horse's heart reaching out to you. Take a little time to absorb the love and peace that comes with it.

Many things can happen when you are in this state of awareness, which provides access to the infinite gateway of learning, for it's an intense, deep conversation. By being heart-to-heart, do you sense who is inside your horse's body? How does it feel to be so connected that you can actually feel in your hand the sum total that is your horse? What do you feel in your heart?

Something that the horse wants you to know will come through during this time. What is it? Are you transported somewhere for a spiritual lesson? See what images or colors arise in your mind's eye in response to your heart speaking. Then ask the horse, "What is your heart's desire?" Explore what you feel and sense as you continue to communicate heart-to-heart.

This is an incredibly moving experience for a horse, too, because everything he or she knows can be placed inside you in that moment. You may not even be aware of what you are being given, but at some point when you most need it in life, it will surface to help you out.

"Heartwarming" is active participation in an unfolding future that depends on us. To that end, horses know that we depend on them to lead us there with eyes, minds, and hearts wide open.

You can do this exercise at any time to enhance your relationship with horses or to seek knowledge about yourself or your horse. The heart mind can help you with anything that you need to know. I find it the most moving two-way healing experience, which is not possible with any other being. It enables me to become united with the paradox of innocence and wisdom that is at the heart of every equine.

Heart-to-heart with horses

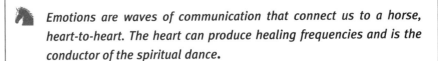

Emotions are waves of communication that connect us to a horse, heart-to-heart. The heart can produce healing frequencies and is the conductor of the spiritual dance.

All cells "listen" to whispers in their environment, including heart vibrations. Each of the two trillion cells in your body has as many working parts as a Boeing 747. Cell frequencies will affect others that we come into contact with, especially horses.

The brain is not the sole driver of intuition and the sixth sense; it seems to link to the heart.

There is a resonance between electrical energy going through the heart and around the body; therefore, feeling loved and nurtured is very important for well-being. It is a reason why, as with us, unhappy horses can be more prone to injury or illness, with slower rates of recovery.

All life-forms are in tune with the "earth's heartbeat" resulting from our planet being encased in a layer of electrically charged particles called the ionosphere.

Coherence is a state where heart rhythms, brain waves, and respiration interact and synchronize, becoming resonant and in tune one with the other. When in this state, we are fully and deeply connected with other beings. Through healing interaction with a horse we can become coherent.

When your heart speaks, listen. It is responding to something an equine wants you to know. Don't be intimidated or shamed by other people who do not have your sensitivity.

Only when we look into our heart will we awaken to reality, our vision becoming clear regarding what we need to do for horses as a reciprocal agreement in exchange for what they can teach us about life.

When the thinking mind recognizes the healing heart mind, we explore the abundant tapestry of experience and expression.

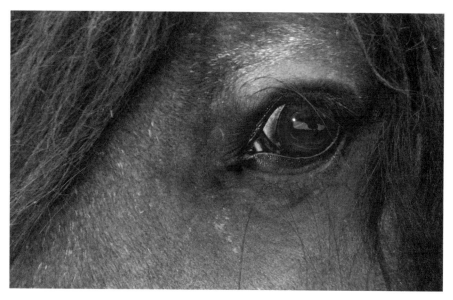

It's important to look into the eyes of horses. They expect this form of interaction because, being social animals, horses want us to look them directly in the eye, as eyes transmit energy from our thoughts and, therefore, eye contact is a means of communication. Staring or looking with eyes that reflect anger or other turmoil will unsettle a horse, whereas eyes with a soft, clear, and loving look will connect us deeply. Researchers have concluded that for altruism (concern and regard for people other than ourselves) to exist, we need to have the ability to see the world through the eyes of others, empathizing with their goals and ideas. Scientists at Duke University Medical Centre in Durham, North Carolina, found that when people are altruistic it is not the "reward centers" of the brain that fire up, but rather the part linked to perception of others' actions.

This suggests that when our agendas are set to one side and we concentrate instead on wanting to help the horse purely for his or her benefit, the more we will understand who this being before us is, because then the part of our brain that interprets the horse's actions comes into play.

The more we give from the heart, the more the mind receives.

The heart is a powerhouse of information

From our heart mind comes the silent knowledge that informs us of our identity and which communicates with the heart mind of horses. The brain mind distracts us, and, therefore, we frequently ignore the horse's subliminal signals. With our heart mind we don't think, we feel the horse, knowing what he or she means us to do, sensing the love and guidance offered. With our head we think that we know the horse and what is happening, but are influenced by scattered thoughts and agendas. When the heart speaks and the mind is still, we hear the horse whispering to our soul.

89

7 Stillness speaks

Having a place of peace means that we can step into it at any time, away from anything that we wish to leave, so we can take stock and replenish ourselves. Stillness is awareness and horses have that in abundance, which is why they can teach it so well. Awareness is not just about what is happening but it *is* us.

In this millennium we have gotten into a situation where we find ourselves short of time and so often neglect to experience the simple pleasures that do us good. Most of us are so focused on multitasking that we whiz through life, jumping from one thing to another. This means scarcely pausing to take a breath, let alone paying attention to what is going on around us or how we are feeling. We are often so busy "doing" that we don't have time to "be." We need a better balance and for that reason it's very beneficial to find the time to ask nothing of a horse other than just to share his or her company, which can result in some priceless moments.

Several such occasions spring to mind; I remember silently infusing myself with the presence of a horse when suddenly the air was full of the most beautiful song as a swallow returning from Africa flew over our heads, singing, "Hello, I'm back, how are you?" I joined the horse in saying, "I'm very happy to see you." There was also the time that a mare pushed her day-old foal towards me with great pride and joy. In these and other such moments I am a privileged party to a parallel world, which exists everywhere that life resonates to the pulse of the universe.

At the same time, a non-resonant hectic pace of life goes on elsewhere, people seeking fulfillment in shops, offices, bars, cafés, theme parks. In our fast society people are pushed and rushed into doing things driven by targets, goals, deadlines, and instant gratification. Days become filled with excitable uproar and often little that is meaningful gets accomplished, with many people suspecting that they are missing something fundamental. In such a state of distraction it can be like trying to make sense of fog. This was a situation I used to find myself in and I'm grateful that nowadays my involvement with horses helps illuminate my thinking; the evolving expansive learning it brings is hugely fulfilling.

> **"**The trilogy of healing, love, and spirituality stems from the stillness deep within us.**"**

Paying attention to silence helps us to slow down and appreciate not only ourselves but the friendships of horses and to be able to hear what they say to us. When struggling to understand something it's useful to become peaceful, for our innate intelligence operates soundlessly. It's surprising how, when a person takes the time to relax and get to know a horse, the horse suddenly becomes "an easier ride" or "better to handle." Confrontation removed, we blend with the equine synergy.

For them to be so in touch with the energy of others, it means that fundamentally horses must be operating through an established center of inner peace. If they did not have this foundation, they would not be able to read us like they do. Even when a horse is unsettled, that self-attunement holds fast, meaning that their information-processing system does not become scrambled.

Inside each of us is a still point, too, a dimension of balanced energy around which multitudes of other energies swirl and from which we can also tune into others. Even during times of crisis our inner sanctuary is there for us to retreat to, and it's OK to feel troubled, unhappy, angry, depressed, grief-stricken, fearful—in fact, it's essential to experience these states in life. It's beneficial to explore the energy of feelings, including mental and emotional pain, and to move with them, extracting what we need. We find out that in doing so we travel forward in our lives. All of us will run a gauntlet of emotions on a regular basis; life is not a continuum of joy. Strength, however, comes from being aware of what's happening and how to deal with it so that we don't lose our way. Unlike the horse, which seems to link naturally to a still point, humans have to make a conscious effort to access this state, and by associating with horses we can aim to absorb their technique.

People sometimes say to me that when they have worries in life they try to be cheerful around their horses so as to not upset them, but I tell them there is no point in acting because you are known to the horse. As empathizers, I believe horses understand the processes that we go through in order to evolve to spiritual health. They help us set aside destructive habits so we can cut a swath through the complications of life and, in doing so, we begin to deal with our conditioning from within.

The opposite to stillness is control, something that results in a lot of unhappiness. Controlling involves following old patterns of what we know and blocks innovation from surfacing. When we let go of controlling tendencies and nurture self-respect, we begin to engender an atmosphere that others can enjoy. The more we negotiate through the resilience that comes from inner stability, the more easily our relationships can develop. We can get out of control mode by reaching inward to our place of peace—it's that easy. Horses do not control by humiliating each other or seeking to make themselves look good at another's expense. They are assertive just enough to establish clear lines of communication and never abuse that role, always caring for each other.

Listening

It's good to listen to silence and absorb it as this helps to awaken the dimension of innermost stillness. In silence, awareness is heightened until we realize the magnificence of who we are, disguised as a human.

Horses are generally placid creatures and they particularly like the sounds of other horses. Silence may be unsettling to humans because as a race we neglect to listen to the cosmos through the spiritual self. Therefore, we fill the world with noise and, due to all the distractions, our sensory expansion is stifled, as is purposeful and productive action. We can't get away from external noise, which corresponds to the inner noise of our thoughts. Maybe it is because we are filled with so much "chatter" that so many people find it uncomfortable to be in a place that is quiet.

Horses have a lot to teach us about inner tranquillity, the equivalent to external silence. Rather than relying on artificial sounds to dull our senses, horses can show us how to appreciate and understand natural impressions. Through being peaceful, our connection to horses is made much stronger due to a cessation of thinking. We then operate on their level of existence, a place of quiescence where there is endless rich opportunity for us to acquire perception and comprehension.

When I invite people to become still inside so that they can experience the energy of their horse as I work, many find this difficult to achieve because of the way that modern life has created tensions that they cannot let go of. However, it's possible to get in touch with the cosmic pulse even when lots of things are happening—we can cut through noise to become aware of the calm above which noise arises. Even when there is external noise we can recognize the space in which sounds arise and, by dropping our resistance, travel into the realms of body/mind/soul congruence. In particular, this is a very useful thing to do when competing or with an inexperienced and traumatized horse. In stillness, problem-solving can be more easily achieved because the focus it instills helps direct words, thoughts, and actions; elements to be fully aware of in any situation that demands attentiveness.

Through applying this concept, Harriet found that making adjust-

> 66 We need a better balance; we are often so busy 'doing' that we don't have time to 'be.' 99

93

ments helped her connect with her horse:

> I would rush in to see Duke before dashing home to attend to the family. Even on weekends when I rode it was hectic and it was a shock to realize that I never properly touched my horse except to put tack on or quickly groom him. The relationship with him has changed beyond all measure now that I have learned to be peaceful through sharing a healing breath, and clearing my mind before touching him. Sharing stillness with my horse has become very healing for me, an aspect that I had not considered might happen.

Sarah has also discovered the benefits of moments of calm. She now often sits with her horse Merlin on warm summer mornings, stroking him while he lies flat out. Through the peace it gives rise to she has changed from being a person who gets stressed if her life is not organized and planned down to the smallest detail, to admitting, "I am learning to

---

Some explanations of stillness

Stillness is an experience wherein a great deal takes place, as the horse knows and shows us. Creating a space within means you can let go of what you don't need in order to expand the essentials, and make room for new concepts. It's a spiritual version of moving out of the way or having a good clear-out so that you can become more vibrantly alive.

Through this expansion you have the potential to see yourself in a new light. As you do so, your view of individuals or groups belonging to all species will alter, leading to a better understanding of them. Knowledge is your power, through which you can make an impact to help improve the lives of others.

Stillness is not "nothingness," absence, or being empty, but a dimension that is deeper and infinitely vaster than thought, and which signposts us towards better understanding of the equine friends in our lives, as well as other partnerships.

Silence is not essential to find stillness within, which is the pure awareness of our consciousness and spirituality.

There are two types of stillness: physical and spiritual. Complete physical stillness cannot be achieved because the body comprises energy that is in perpetual motion. Spiritually we are separate from the physical and all we have to do to activate peace is to become aware of our natural state.

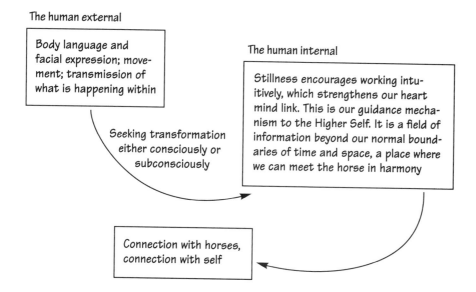

The human external

Body language and facial expression; movement; transmission of what is happening within

Seeking transformation either consciously or subconsciously

The human internal

Stillness encourages working intuitively, which strengthens our heart mind link. This is our guidance mechanism to the Higher Self. It is a field of information beyond our normal boundaries of time and space, a place where we can meet the horse in harmony

Connection with horses, connection with self

Through seeking stillness we go beyond concentrating on what is occurring around us to achieving a balance with our internal world. This, in turn, helps us connect with horses.

extract meaning from each moment."

Horses often become quiet around children and I believe that this could be either partly or wholly because children can have an inner calmness about them, which horses like. Agitated horses can become docile in response to a child's uncomplicated composure and open mind.

Becoming aware

We can find ourselves swept away by overwhelming feelings, thoughts, worries, pressures, and responsibilities. As well as draining our energy, being pressurized in this way will have a ripple effect in any encounter we have with others, including horses.

Be mindful

Mindfulness helps us to let go of stressful thoughts by increasing our awareness of the present moment. By focusing on breathing we can stop the mind from racing and distracting the horse from what we would like him or her to do. Using phrases such as, "I am feeling peaceful" or "I feel happy" can help change the breathing rate, assisting in becoming more mindful. Being mindful helps improve the associations that we form in any sphere.

When we relax into each moment our senses sharpen and things take on a new perspective. This helps us to sense what a horse is thinking and feeling, resulting in us either taking a different course of action or accepting what is happening without assuming that it is a conflict.

Take five plus one

The five senses of sight, hearing, smell, taste, and touch all have something to add to the enjoyment of each day, and when we make a conscious effort to use them we fully experience life. The intuitive sixth sense can help give us direction, leading to making decisions that are better all around. Horses continually operate through all their senses and when we are fully alert we can connect with them at the same level.

Think positively

> **When we delve within and look for pleasure in simple things, rather than believing that only possessions or accolades bring happiness, we can start to process an inner calmness that the horse beams back to us, magnifying the peace.**

Whatever the mind expects, it will find; whatever we focus on will become the center of our attention—a good reason to be always aware of what we are giving our attention to. We move in the direction in which we think and the horse follows us there.

Make a commitment to yourself

Making a commitment to yourself means aiming to live your own truth; in doing so, life becomes an exploration of ever-increasing enlightenment. Through making a self-commitment you find your power, but this does not mean becoming a different person. Rather it involves reacting in a different way to stimuli, opportunities, and situations. The stillness created through commitment can be used to redirect us away from behaviors or habits that do not serve any useful purpose. The horse nods wisely when we reach this stage and puts out the welcome mat.

Improving relationships

The purpose of a spiritual teacher—and the horse falls into that category, of course—is not to teach anything new in the conventional sense, but to help us to move beyond that which separates us from what we already know and, by doing so, to uncover our identity. In revealing this dimension we find our place and, therefore, our purpose in life. Peace and stillness go hand in hand and lead to a suspension of what is not important in exchange for harmony. When we are able to be still, peace reigns.

The following guidelines on sacred space meditation are intended to help develop your capacity to quieten the mind, with the benefit of improving equine relationships, thus stimulating an increased awareness of their guidance. Meditating with a horse is best done outdoors, because the horse should be able to move away from you at will and thereby be more relaxed. I suggest keeping the other side of a fence to a horse, so that you can close your eyes safe in the knowledge that you and your horse each have your own space.

Explore what's there

Breathing deeply, listen, feel, and absorb the goodness and the power that is all around you. Feel the energy of your horse reaching out and connecting with you.

Place your attention on being inside your body, focusing on it completely. Then take the time to invite the horse to absorb you into his or her body, so that you get a feeling of horse sense. Finally, imagine both of you blending into one so there is no beginning or end to either of you. Together you *become* the universe.

Open your mind

Meditation can offer a perception of release and a greater perspective on life. Clearing the mind isn't always easy because overwhelming niggling thoughts can take over. Contemplation with contented horses is very helpful because their minds are uncluttered and we can draw on that energy.

Look at the bigger picture

Creating sacred space helps develop compassionate sentiments, benefiting others.

Make it a ritual with your horse

Meditating together regularly can help improve immune function and reduce anxiety, lifting moods.

Life is a grand adventure in which we explore the unknown, but which is recognized by horses. It's a rewarding journey to make together.

> **"**The heart yearns for us to be still so that it can liberate our senses.**"**

8 In the round

Being a social animal, the horse is biologically programmed to cooperate with us and to form long-term permanent bonds. Humans, too, are social creatures and in this respect we share common ground.

Building mutual respect within a horse's natural system of learning and socializing is very rewarding. Of course, this can take a long time but then our whole lifetime is for learning about a great many things, comprising many stages. These days, a human failing is to try to fast-track everything. Probably one of the reasons for gadget popularity is the demand for instant results, but the paradox is that this pressure can, in the long term, produce disappointment and disillusionment.

While horses respond instantly in some respects, a demand for quick results may not have the desired effect or be of benefit to the horse, or even to ourselves in the long term. The horse is always disappointed with those who do not "walk the talk," saying one thing but being incongruent, such as advocating natural horse techniques but then using pressure halters, hobbles, or flooding methods, causing emotional and/or physical pain. Of course I'm not saying that people who use gadgets do not love horses, just that there are preferable ways, based on sound research. All aids, including saddles, bits, bridles, halters, ropes, and our bodies, have the potential to cause harm and this is something we can helpfully be aware of. Horses know the truth in any situation and putting ourselves in their shoes in whatever we undertake with them will lead us to knowing what that reality is.

In the same way that it is for us, when adrenaline in horses is up, learning is down. Therefore, understanding what produces conflict and what induces calmness in horses is going to make a big difference to our education. Australian zoologist, ethologist, and rider Dr. Andrew McLean has lectured on the fact that by applying training methods that are not commensurate with a horse's psychology, his or her optimal learning will be diminished. There is a condition termed "learned help-lessness" whereby a horse is forced into a state where it becomes completely stressed and has to surrender its will, thus feeling totally help-less. Dr. McLean has noted that stressed horses are slow learners because stress causes cortisol and prolactin to be pumped into their brains, inducing brain atrophy. This is going to affect the performance of any horse and should be of interest to trainers, riders, and competitors glob-ally. It means reviewing management/training systems, and making changes to stop stress from arising.

Dr. McLean has also lectured that "clear and consistent signals/responses have the greatest influence on anxiety levels, and training the horse to be completely obedient to light aids is the key to relaxed coop-eration." Correct handling and training of the young horse are vitally important for the horse to be able to relate with confidence to people as he or she goes through life. Problems that a horse may display, at what-ever age, are related in some way to pain/discomfort, breakdown in communications, or management/feeding/lifestyle/work. The repercus-sions can reverberate for a long time, even a lifetime, particularly as horses are commonly passed around numerous homes. A horse may frequently not show stress, internalizing it or being too fearful to show it, and those that do are frequently labeled bad or difficult when that is not the case.

We cannot achieve a good connection with a horse that is not feeling relaxed about life, just as when we are feeling stressed we are not in the best frame of mind to form friendships ourselves. It's within our power to eliminate stress in the lives of horses and the fact that so much persists is testament to the amount of help that needs to be given to them. In helping horses we then also understand more about our own limitations and how to overcome them. The most honest feedback will come from a horse that is free to express individuality and is at peace. By being comfortable with that scenario we reflect our ability to give and take in relationships generally. In terms of seeking a deep connection, this surely has to be the way forward towards kinship, which is true horsemanship.

Horses enlist us to join them in the alliance to further good manners, for herds are dependent on such necessities. Good manners mean respecting each being, recognizing idiosyncratic merits as qualities we can learn from in some form, and that interdependence is vital for survival.

Doing what is right for the horse

For the horse's sake we must all take stock and do what is right for him or her, and that means setting aside much of what we have been doing so far. Ethologist and lecturer in animal behavior at Southampton University, U.K., Dr. Deborah Goodwin states that:

> Human culture has benefited greatly through its interactions with horses over the last 6,000 years, and our history would have been very different without them. We are now developing knowledge to eliminate some of the detrimental consequences that domestication has placed on the horse. The horse is powerless to implement these advances; that responsibility is entirely ours.

Dr. Goodwin has undertaken studies investigating what head lowering in equines, commonly taken to mean a submissive response, actually means. In herds it is used as a distance-reducing signal between approaches made by friendly horses. With human training methods, such as lunging and in the round pen, it is a signal horses use to show that they would like to approach the person and do something else. This is a good reason to move away from the myth of head lowering being a sign that the horse wants to submit to us, thus leading to a spiral of escalating misconception.

No wonder the horse frequently appears frustrated at our lack of understanding of their communications, viewing us as an unintelligent species compared with equines.

> **"** If we want horses to give us partnership and friendship, then we should not take their health from them. **"**

Personality types

By having some inkling of horse personality types, we can get a better picture of why individual horses can display completely different responses and reactions to things. This helps us in whatever we undertake, otherwise we can literally go around in circles making the same mistakes over and over again. When we look at the whole package, it's not just about horses, it's about life, learning, and love.

The following helpful guidelines were drawn up by Dr. Carey Williams, Extension Specialist in Equine Management at Rutgers University, New Jersey. However, horses are not "tick boxes" any more than humans are and it must be taken into consideration that breeding, weaning, feeding, physical/emotional comfort, age, and lifestyle all contribute to behavior and expression.

Demonstrative, confident horse

- Lets you know when he or she is stressed.

- Bucks, kicks, bites, is very curious, mouthy, a troublemaker.

Demonstrative, fearful horse

- Worries about everything.

- Shies the first time he or she sees things and needs time to relax.

Passive, confident horse

- Usually wonders, "What's everyone worried about?"

- Not normally easily stressed, internalizes stress, shows little change, even when stressed.

- Usually is the last one in the field to take off running if something appears out of the woods.

Passive, fearful horse

- Wants to please.

- Seems willing to do anything, but will tighten muscles and lips when stressed.

- Won't show fear until pushed over the limit.

Some things to remember

The horse asks us to remember the following things:

- Horses are capable of conscious thought. Therefore, we need to tap into their minds to encourage them to do what we ask. This way they work with us, and without fear.

- A horse may be in a trained state or an instinctive state. Whatever the state of the horse, it's important to work with natural behavior and without time restraints. Horses do not wear watches or keep a diary. A genuine horseman or woman has all the time in the world to form a bond.

Every horse is an individual, so he or she should not be subjected to fixed methods or programs. Training and schooling must be flexible and adaptable, not least because horses change as we do. Becoming stuck in dogma is not productive in terms of building meaningful relationships with either horses or other humans.

All horses are not suitable for all things. Problems occur due to our asking something that a horse is not emotionally, mentally, or physically capable of doing.

Horses with development issues teach us completely different things from those that have had a stable background; the most obvious lesson being that of cause and effect. Interfering with nature creates imbalance that affects everyone and everything.

In the training of horses there is frequent emphasis on discipline, yet the necessity and importance of our own self-discipline needs to be appreciated so that horses do not suffer through anything that is being asked of them.

Images or talk of "the perfect horse doing the perfect thing" can influence what we do and in emulating others, the horse can end up an unfortunate and unwilling partner. In reality, the perfect horse is one that loves us and as they all inherently want to do that, we learn that all horses are perfect.

Round pens

Round pens are not a modern invention: in fact, they appear to date back to ancient Roman times when they were called "gyros." Natalie Waran, Professor of Animal Welfare at Unitec, New Zealand, has written that the Roman gyros were used to enclose horses so they were manageable and then to keep them moving, resulting in fatigue, which made them easier to mount. Commonly a place to school horses, a round pen can also be used as an exercise area to restrict movement after injury or illness. Sometimes it is used as a place for excited, over-confined horses to let off steam because they cannot gallop or play with other horses (although it is bad practice to get a horse into that state of agitation in

Terminologies

There can be confusion about terminologies relating to horses. To help with clarity, these are my definitions:

Natural horsemanship *includes providing a horse with a herd lifestyle and foraging, and can include handling—however, gadgets and artificial aids are not part of the horse's natural world. The words "natural" and "horsemanship" cannot be owned by a method or individual and when combined into the phrase "natural horsemanship" mean providing the things that a horse naturally requires or in terms of handling, understanding horse/herd behavior.*

Equine ethology *is the scientific study of animal behavior from an evolution and adaptive perspective. It can teach us about social interaction, feeding habits, species communication, habitat, and how/why things go wrong, resulting in stereotypic behaviors and training difficulties.*

Equitation science *includes a combination of behavior science, psychology, and veterinary disciplines. Horses have not evolved to carry people on their backs; therefore, at the stage that we ride, we need to use a multidisciplinary approach to help us understand how to do the right things.*

Many management/training systems used today have their origins in the past, before disciplines such as ethology, comparative psychology, and equitation science emerged. These disciplines offer an understanding of horse nature and physiology, and how we can prevent problems with horses, or overcome them if they do occur. Holistic management offers the best opportunity to harmonize with the horse's innate nature and help the domestic horse to be healthy—mentally, emotionally, and physically.

the first place). In coaching/therapy workshops, it may be used as a space for horse and human to interact with each other.

I have often seen training take place in a round pen or using gadget-based methods, both of which make me uncomfortable. Frequently horses in such situations show defensive strategies—ears back, tautness around the mouth, staring eyes, flight response—or they show reactive responses, threatening to strike with forelimbs or turning to threaten a kick. I don't see the point in instigating any of these responses when the aim is to build a relationship based on integrity. Why not free-school and explore language around the concept of "your soul shares equality with my soul"? In the wild state that is fundamental to the horse's psyche, there is no equivalent to the round pen; there is therefore nothing natural about it and it alerts equines to the consequences of being trapped by a predator.

Heather Simpson from the Natural Animal Centre, Wales, does not support the use of round pens for training because she feels that chasing a horse around is nothing to do with engendering love and trust but everything to do with fear and intimidation. Heather has written numerous articles explaining that round pens sometimes lead to "frozen watchfulness" or hypervigilance and that this ironically can create follow-me behavior. When these articles were published, they generated hundreds of thousands of website hits as people recognized a universal truth in what was being said in them, relieved that their own discomfort had a scientific label. Heather states: "There is no logic to using round pens in training; why would I want to chase a horse away from me with a stick and a rope when I really want him to come up close and love me?"

One owner called me out because she was worried that the relationship with her much-loved mare was damaged and wanted me to communicate how sorry she was at being coerced into taking part in a session at her riding club. Her horse had been impossible to send away, just wanting to come to her. In hindsight, she said it was a pointless exercise because they had already bonded and it only resulted in confusion and sadness for both. With any form of training or riding, people may have the wrong idea about what they are trying to achieve and they can so easily cause distress. After all, the horse cannot shout, "This is no fun and I don't want to play!", so work can become forced and signals to stop ignored. Trust then goes out of the window and there is no basis for a connection. Whatever space we choose to make a horse share with us (for enclosure is not a horse's choice), the horse must feel relaxed and not be wishing that it had never met us. It's easy to overlook this when the ego inflates.

Discussing horse-human interaction with Linda Kohanov, herself an experienced trainer, she offered this advice:

Any enclosure—round, square, oval, rectangular, stall, stable, arena or pasture—can be used to foster greater connection between horse and human or it can be misused out of ignorance, ego, and dominance, leading to physical, emotional, or even spiritual injury. The most immediate danger regarding the round pen in particular is the way in which it has been promoted as a quick-fix "miraculous" training tool through some rather extensive yet supremely superficial press, mostly through the "horse whisperer" or "natural horsemanship" phenomenon.

105

Horse owners who have no knowledge of the subtleties of equine body language attend a workshop or buy a training DVD by a popular clinician. They go home and try to replicate the superficial mechanics of the training method without recognizing equine signs of increasing stress.

Also many round pens have mediocre if not downright terrible footing and are much too small for a horse to move around in without undue stress on the joints. Round pens under fifty feet should only be used as reflective spaces to explore connection off lead through gentle voluntary movements. I personally find square pens less desirable, not because I can't move the horse in that context, but because symbolically the square reminds me of rigid box-like thinking, while the circle symbolically reminds me of wholeness. The main context where I choose to use a round pen involves teaching people how to engage directed movement with the horse, whereby free techniques are taught as part of a much larger vocabulary of "dance moves." This leads to improvisatory reactions, often to music, between horse and human. First a person is coached in recognizing body language cues, energetic, emotional, and spatial needs and holding safe boundaries with a horse walking alongside.

This method of teaching helps to eliminate much confusion and misunderstanding both for humans and horses.

Safe space

Horses are intelligent animals, and aware that relationships are not made by running around in circles. When humans indulge in this activity it is for their benefit only. While this technique may work for some combinations of horses/humans, it is not the way the horse desires to establish friendship and leadership.

Ethologist, coach, and human-animal interactions specialist Mary Ann Simonds writes in her book *Horse Wisdom*:

Today many people are wishing to go beyond controlling their horse and want to understand, learn from, and form a strong friendship with their horse. This requires giving up some old ideas and models of horse training and moving into a more horse-orientated non-stressful technique of forming a relationship based on trust, safety, and nurturing, instead of obedience, control, and submissiveness.

A horse wants to find a safe space to stand in where there is no threat and it can belong to the herd. If you as a human can create a safe nurturing environment, then the horse will usually want to join your herd . . . a horse by nature does not want to be chased and run around if it can stand still next to you. Watching a fearful horse run around in circles may be entertaining to humans, but does not offer the simplest way to build a friendship with a horse. It is far better for the horse to watch the human communicate in the horse's language of play and space taking.

Horses are feeling animals and when chased or moved around in circles, they become anxious and vigilant regarding their safety—they cannot help it. Is that what we are looking for in our search for connection, or do we want a horse to feel contented with what we ask, desiring us as companions? For humans who want to do the right thing by the horse, developing a deep and lasting bond, and to fully understand all horses per se, training methods that the horse actually prefers are the right way to go.

In her DVD *My Space, Your Space, Understanding Horse Culture*, Mary Ann advocates exercises based on natural horse behavior, which take place in a good-sized area to develop spatial awareness between horse and human. She also reminds people that energy can be used to influence the movement of horses, saying, "The horse easily picks up various thoughts and feelings, not only by watching body language but by sensing your energy."

> **"** The healing horse must first be healed by us if we are to fully reap the benefit of his or her wisdom. **"**

Exploring the edges

Stepping out of our comfort zone is often what helps us to achieve the seemingly impossible. Whenever I have stepped or been forced out of my comfort zone it has always been a frightening experience, but when viewed in hindsight those times challenged me to move to a place that I would not otherwise have risen to. I explored this topic with rider-sport psychologist Liz Morrison. In her article entitled "Holding the Space and Yet Exploring the Edges," Liz includes the following observations:

One of the interesting points about working with metaphor is to notice the different levels it works at. Often people are using the round pen to do the sort of coaching with horses that I have explored and developed. Yet, no matter what the metaphor, I now believe that this is, by its very nature, a restricting space. One of the points I am exploring is the importance of "safe spaces," and the paradigm is that there cannot be true exploration in a contained, known area. By definition, all one can do is go to the edge, the established boundaries.

When you take the horse into the round pen, the whole process of driving it out to the edge is stressful to the horse, creating a level of anxiety that is less than helpful to start with. It would be interesting to see a session where the participants ran around the edge with the horses and considered what it felt like from that perspective. Confusing, not knowing what was expected, trying to get approval? Probably! Much like the treadmill, which is the common metaphor of the modern workplace, going around and around is certainly pointless, often frustrating—and stressful. So, from the research I have completed, I believe that little radical change or insight can actually be gained in the round pen. True exploration comes from stepping out of the confines and really exploring what lies beyond them. Often that feels lonely or unsafe, even vulnerable, and that is the nature of true learning, enabling profound change. Sure, when in a large square space the horses may run away from you. "What does that tell you? How can you 'be' so that the horses want to connect with you as a true leader?" I ask people.

A round pen maintains the subliminal power relationship that is evident in many incongruent situations. The horse will be looking for signals that give reassurance, or it has to submit to tiredness and acknowledge the "leader." The horse running around the outside until it submits, the person in the center—commanding, controlling—is not an attractive picture. The power relationship is an unspoken feature in many, many relationships. Yet true change cannot be considered without addressing it. For command and control will not work in the chaotic, rapidly changing environment that we are starting to face up to in the twenty-first century. Just as in the story of the emperor's new clothes, at some point it is necessary to step up to the facts.

The new leadership that is needed in the workplace, in families, in society is about honesty, leading from deeply held congruent values. It is often described as humility and intuition. Internationally renowned trainer Mark Rashid describes it as passive leadership, with horses selecting a natural leader where they can be calm and build relationships rather than be chased and dominated. Instead of using the round pen I therefore choose to work with horses in a large

space for reflective work. Usually for comfort with corporate groups, in case of inclement weather, this is an indoor school (arena). However, rich explorations also happen with small groups of horses in their fields and paddocks.

As a person who is passionate about allowing the horse freedom to express personality, intelligence, and emotion, all of this makes a lot of sense to me. When a horse is truly allowed to be a horse, is when we get to know him or her. Then, our own spirit responds by being able to read horses as astutely as they read us. This moves us away from our box-like thinking and fixed ideas, enabling us to better understand the individual that the horse is.

Lunging focus

Modern training and exercising of horses is focused on the use of the lunge line and this is frequently to the detriment of the horse. It is a misnomer to say that lunging builds a "connection" with the horse, because the human controls the movements and direction of the horse and problems frequently arise through this. In theory, expert lunging improves suppleness and muscle development, but there has to be a point where trick movements and fatigue are observed and the session ended.

Horses can become distressed for a variety of reasons, but typically the horse will suffer in silence. If the horse reacts by flattening the ears, stopping, rearing, bucking, or trying to come towards the handler (which is effectively saying, "Please stop this"), then he or she is labeled difficult; even worse, the handler may work the horse for longer to "teach it a lesson."

Lunging is used by veterinarians to show up lameness patterns and that in itself demonstrates the extra loading that going around in circles produces. As regards the use of side reins, ostensibly to create a bend in the horse's neck, evidence shows that where side reins result in a too low or too high head carriage, the back locks up and hind limb propulsion is affected, also creating abnormal musculature.

World-renowned veterinary physiotherapist and musculoskeletal expert Amanda Sutton asks her clients not to lunge their horses for several reasons:

- Young horses are not balanced or coordinated and being made to work in circles is physically stressful for them.

- With older horses, lunging creates excessive loading on joints and soft tissues, which are already compromised.

- With any horse, the use of schooling aids while lunging also adds load and changed posture. Often the horse uses trick movements to try to remain comfortable. To recognize this, an understanding of correct horse movement is needed by a handler and most do not have this skill.

- Research clearly shows that head and neck posture influences low back flexibility and hind limb propulsion.

- If we change the horse's movement by influencing it with lunging and schooling aids, we need to be aware of the potential negative effects on the way that the horse will move.

- Dysfunctional gait patterns can become more entrenched, and postural and supporting muscles do not actually become developed by lunge line techniques in these cases.

In addition to the reasons above, these techniques can lead to neck/head muscle spasms and pain and/or headaches. The practice also restricts shoulder movement. If using this method to correct or achieve a certain way of going, great care is needed. It is vital to be able to assess if the horse can do what you are asking without adoption of aberrant movement patterns. Amanda instead advocates long reining, loose schooling, and in-hand work to exercise a horse without a rider.

Other methods that can cause physical injury and damage are rein back, sudden stops, spins and short turns, making a horse stand on the hind legs, and over-bent necks. There are numerous other areas of misuse, including working horses and ponies so severely that they become lathered, treating them like jumping machines, and many stunts/tricks. It takes only three minutes to trigger repetitive stress injury or occupational overuse syndrome and equines suffer from these too.

Equine chiropractor Dr. Sean B. Wall further explains:

> The horse is a prey animal which flees in a straight line. Through evolution, the horse's lumbosacral (lower back/pelvic area) junction is constructed to allow flexion/extension and prevent rotation. Lunging, in particular tight circles, as well as twisting, training, or ridden movements, can overstress the horse's lumbosacral region, causing chronic discomfort and dysfunction.

66 To enable the best rapport to take place, we should not be forever reminding a horse that he is prey and we are predator. That is a lesson in itself. **99**

The right thing

A woman called me to ask advice about her son's pony, which was being treated for anemia, and due to lethargy "had to be pushed really hard to complete an important cross-country competition." It's torture for an equine to do anything but rest when below par for whatever reason, especially when carrying a hassling rider. Nothing is worth the sacrifice of another's well-being. It's essential to consider another being's needs and seek the best possible advice if we are unsure about anything. When we try to force others, of what- ever species, to join us or perform for us, it rarely has a happy outcome because they become resentful and we actually push them away. That then sets up a cycle of insecurity and loss of confidence, the other party being viewed as unpleasant or stubborn. When we are empathic, other beings are more likely to say, "I like you, can I be your friend?"

A positive thing to do if we want guidance on whether we are doing the right thing, in any aspect of horsemanship, is to ask, "If I was this horse, right now, and another person was doing what I am, would I feel relaxed or fearful? Would I love them or hate them?" and, "If I had to swap places with this horse, would I like what was being done to me?"

The answer coming back from the horse can be sobering. If we want horses to give us partnership and friendship, we should not take their health from them.

Redirection

While we may have romantic notions of our ancestors and their relationships with horses, prior to domestication there was freedom for horse and human to get to know each other without constraint. When we move full circle into a position of autonomy there is rediscovery of a magical connection that I believe our soul and the horse's soul yearn to rekindle. Depending on their experiences, most horses will be happy to relate to us. Sometimes this can happen instantly; at other times, we can struggle to make a connection, either because it is the wrong combination or the horse needs something that we have not considered.

> 66 Horses show up our strengths and weaknesses with blatant honesty. 99

Once at a gathering I watched a trainer work with some young horses. He normally used a round pen, but when he turned up at the venue, theirs was waterlogged. He tried his methods with the horses at liberty in a large square space and they just didn't work—the horses were reluctant to get close to him, instead dashing around all over the place. When he went for a break, another man who had been watching, and who had little horse-handling experience, slipped under the fence to clean up the surface. This person had no agenda and very quickly a young horse wandered over, curious as to what was happening, before following the man around as he worked. The trainer returned, the other man left, and the horse ran away. Everyone was amused, apart from the flustered trainer.

On another occasion, I attended a demonstration by a therapist during which a non-horsey woman was invited into a round pen with a pony that had never been in one before; a potentially dangerous scenario. The trembling pony took the center as the safest place to be, from where he could observe all around him. The woman was then asked to move the pony to the outside of the pen using only her thoughts. However, the flight/fight instinct was overriding everything in the pony's world, so he stuck to the middle ground, turning his back threateningly if the woman stepped in from the outer edge of the pen, and she became increasingly nervous. Eventually, the therapist called it a day; horse and human were mirroring confusion and fear and this pointless exercise resulted in two unhappy individuals leaving the demonstration disconnected from each other, having learned nothing of worth. Repercussions for a horse as well as the human must always be taken into consideration in any type of work as it will affect future interactions, which may cause uncertainties to become established or even phobias.

- It is possible to influence a horse's movements using intention (via our thoughts), as discussed elsewhere in this book. But if we are not aware of every detail, both on the seen and unseen levels, then what is in the foreground of our perception may be an illusion.

- The term "natural horsemanship" can be used with anything, even if a method or system is unnatural to a horse. Therefore, a better way is to consider whether something is inhumane or humane. Is it domination or partnership? Are the horse's emotions/thoughts/feelings being ignored or is he/she being respected as an individual sentient being?

- When we consider matters from the perspective of the whole, including the way of the horse interacting with the human way, a shift takes place, bringing enlightened perception to the foreground of our awareness. This, in turn, characterizes a redirection in our way of thinking.

- By slowing down enough to start to understand the correlation between our frustrations or happiness and our way of doing things, we encounter the authentic whole rather than purely a concept of what we think we are.

- The horse teaches us to see our handprint on all of our actions. With this recognition we can redirect our way of being, away from conditioning to spontaneity and a resonance with all life-forms.

9 The healing power of horses—true stories

Equines of all ages and types can lead us to a place of healing. The following stories represent the wide variety of cases that I come across.

Renoir and Emily

Away at competitions Renoir was difficult to ride, while at home he behaved impeccably. The best had been done for the pony, as he had been checked for pain and saddle fit, and his rider, fifteen-year-old Emily, was experienced and well taught due to both her parents being respected trainers.

The first time that I met Renoir, Emily was at school so her mother Alex was with him, and tuning in I felt as though I suddenly couldn't breathe properly, then my breathing came in short quick bursts. Alex explained how this related to Renoir; at competitions he seemed to freeze and at the end of the test would be hyperventilating.

I needed to work with Emily and Renoir as a team to get to the root of the problem, so I returned to meet Emily and learned from her that Renoir "became dull" at competitions. Emily confirmed, too, how she had always felt disconnected from Renoir; it was as if they didn't understand what each was thinking or wanted to do. She ventured that it wasn't a case of not liking each other, but that they somehow didn't gel and rather than just give up on the pony or beat him into submission it was important to her to identify what was actually wrong.

"There's something I'm missing," Emily said. The final straw had come in an international dressage competition, with three days of tests. Renoir veered between being relaxed and concentrating and being erratic and tense. It was time for me to connect girl and pony.

My informant as to the nature of the problem was, of course, the pony, because only he knew the truth of the situation, humans being less competent at global understanding. Renoir told me that he was affected by Emily's inner being. When they rode in front of other people he knew that she needed approval from them and in doing so her breathing changed; without realizing it she became tense and held her breath, which was why he did the same. The pony was, in fact, mirroring his rider, her tension going through every fiber of his body. *He* could not breathe properly because *she* was not breathing properly, making it very difficult for him to move fluidly, which was why he looked so robotic on those occasions. At home, of course, Emily had no spectators and so relaxed.

Then Renoir communicated that while Emily needed approval from her peers and judges, he actually needed approval from her. Because that was not forthcoming he felt lost and unsupported; he needed to be praised, no matter what he did, and wanted to be loved for himself, not his achievements. This is what Emily was missing—the fact that Renoir needed a partner on his back, and the lack of this was why he froze. He felt alone, sensing that Emily's mind was with the people outside the arena and not connected to him.

I suggested that when Emily rode she concentrated fully on Renoir, saying from her mind: "I approve of everything that you do." She was not to ask for anything from Renoir, simply to keep sending love, which he would take huge comfort from, giving him the confidence he needed. Having explained this I needed to put Emily energetically in touch with Renoir, to enable her to communicate directly with him. As I felt the tell-tale shift in energy state, the pony closed his eyes and sighed and my hands became hot, seemingly magnetized to his neck. Looking across at Emily, her eyes were also shut and her lips were soundlessly moving, as though she was engaged in conversation with someone, responding to things said. Of course she was—that "someone" was Renoir. After a while, Emily took a deep breath and, exhaling, said, "It makes sense." Renoir had explained how he felt, what he needed Emily to do to help him, and not only had she listened, but she had also understood.

A few weeks later we met up again to discuss what had transpired since my visit and I was pleased to hear that Renoir appeared much more relaxed and when out hacking was full of sparkle and *joie de vivre*. They had been to some competitions, which had gone well—in fact, Renoir was even OK about traveling in the truck whereas before he would buck when being loaded. It was as though he now wanted to go and do some work. Due to the previous lack of connection in his relationship with Emily, Renoir's energy had gotten buried and he had lost his enjoyment of life—now his personality had reemerged and they were a team. Emily told me:

It was a very odd experience that day. I didn't feel myself, although I don't know how to describe it. I was in a heightened state of concentration, deeply drawn in to Renoir and not really aware of what was going on around me. Suddenly everything became clear about what he felt. *I actually felt it myself.* The solution then fell into place. That day I became as one with Renoir because I had experienced his thoughts and emotions. Since then, when riding I forget about other people watching and am conscious of encouraging Renoir instead of telling him what to do. I say to him, "It's OK, you can do this," and he seems at peace with me. It's made a huge difference and I feel so close to him now. Last week a judge who knows us well came up and told me that our partnership was the most established she had seen at the whole competition. She said that we were really connected; I was glowing with pride for both of us.

Shortly after this meeting I came across a similar situation of a horse affected by the mind state of the rider. Dime, a western riding horse, was called a one-in-a-million soul mate by his rider Daniella. Tuning into Dime I began to see the world through his eyes—I felt worried about the person on my back, for the rider was tense, had a racing heartbeat, and was overconcerned about the people watching and what they were thinking. I felt protective and blamed them for upsetting her, so I wanted to chase them away. When I passed this information on to Daniella, she told me that at competitions Dime would freak out to such an extent that his usual trick was to attack the judges, rushing at them with ears back and teeth bared. It was very embarrassing!

She admitted to feeling very nervous when she rode under certain circumstances and I explained about the dynamics of horse-human relationships and how Dime would know this. It was a revelation for Daniella and from that day on everything changed due to her adopting a new mind-set. Horse and rider had a much better connection, with Daniella feeling that they were more in tune. The horse responded to the most subtle aids, such as going forward on an in-breath and stopping on an out-breath, like a flowing dance. Their instructor, who did not know of my visit, said that there had suddenly been a huge improvement in their teamwork. When Daniella explained why, he said, "I never knew you got nervous, you never showed it." We can hide anything we want to from other people but *never* from a horse; we are naked before them.

If a horse or pony does well at home but at competitions things go wrong, then the rider could well be the problem. The thoughts of others watching us should not be paramount, because the horse or pony is the only one listening to what we think. Making inner changes can result in a lot of success and fun.

Bronwen and Jo

When everything seems bleak and hopeless, a horse entering our lives can work a miracle. At the age of fifteen, Jo found herself suffering from anorexia and bulimia due to an extreme lack of self-esteem. Over the years she saw numerous psychiatrists and spent long periods in psychiatric units, all to no avail. As an adult Jo still considered herself a failure and a bad person, incapable of achieving anything.

Then one day everything changed: the messenger of hope was a brown Welsh cob called Bronwen. The horse arrived after Jo's son had been given a small pony that no one else wanted and Jo recognized that he could not live alone, so she acquired Bronwen as a companion for him. Jo had no horse knowledge and launched herself into research as to how to do the best for her new family. Instinctively, she knew that everything had to be as natural as possible and to concentrate on working in harmony with horse behavior rather than trying to bend the horse's will to human ideas. Previously, Jo's only experience of seeing people handle horses involved hitting, shouting, or dragging them around.

Things did not, however, get off to a good start because Jo's lack of confidence and uncertainty made Bronwen very anxious; she is a highly sensitive horse who can detect the tiniest doubts or tensions in people and Jo had plenty of both. It dawned on Jo, however, that she was adversely affecting the mare, with Bronwen trying desperately to communicate that Jo had to deal with her own issues before going anywhere near her. However, in typically human fashion, Jo battled on regardless, with more of the same negativity in her attitude until Bronwen became hysterical. She napped, spun round, or ran away when Jo went to bring her in from the paddock and, if Jo had her on a rope, pulled it out of her hands and galloped off.

They reached a deadlock until Jo found help with the right people to help her understand the nature of horses. These trainers showed Jo how to interact with Bronwen as another member of the herd would and how a horse views the world. Through this Jo learned about the parallels of human actions and reactions, such that her lessons took on a depth and clarity that she had not imagined possible—daily revelations spilled out in front of her. She learned that horses highlight human deficiencies and weaknesses by their phenomenal perception, which becomes a healing process. However, it took several more years for Jo to fully overcome the deeply seated insecurities that had plagued most of her life, but along the way it was Bronwen who helped her take each step by her incredible horse guidance. Throughout her journey to recovery, Bronwen never tried to take advantage of Jo's weaknesses; she simply reacted to them, pointing out that they were destructive both to herself and others.

In turning her life around, Jo has made big changes, including leaving her marriage because it was wrong for her, and is taking steps to set up a business in equine involvement therapy whereby she can help others struggling with their lives, with, of course, Bronwen's help. Jo sees all of this as proof of her complete recovery because she is now self-sufficient, without fear, and feels strong and positive. She confirms:

> At the heart of any healing is the desire to be healed. My extreme lack of confidence and self-hatred was so inward-looking. I knew that I needed to look out beyond myself to be healed and that is where the horse's magic lies. The more that you do this and listen to what they are offering, the more the healing process can begin. After a life of self-punishment I allowed myself that reward—horses teach that you are worthwhile because the rewards they give are worth achieving.

Jo describes Bronwen as the most wonderful creature ever created and says that she is beautiful both in terms of looks and her loving heart. Bronwen now has a son called Winner who will follow in his mother's footsteps to help more people in the future recover from the traumas of being human. This generosity of spirit makes horses the embodiment of perfect and forgiving love.

Joan, Roxy, and Sue

It was, of course, an equine with whom I shared yet another profound lesson; however, it was not a horse or pony this time, but a donkey called Joan. The aged donkey was grieving for her companion Roxy, a horse who had been put to sleep by the vet a week before.

Sue, the vet, was in fact the owner of both donkey and horse, and it had been a hugely brave act to help her much-loved horse to a world of eternal peace. Sue had chosen a lovely spring day, a calm window in a week of blustery wet weather. With the sun shining and the birds singing, the omens were good and Sue made a bed of straw to one side of the paddock. Roxy was happy to munch away on the straw and it was so very peaceful when the medication opened a gate for Roxy to journey through to heaven. Joan was let out of her stable to look around and, in fact, ignored her friend's body, strolling around the fields looking for tasty young shoots to eat. However, even though Joan was putting on a brave face, things were clearly amiss because after that she did not want to go into the paddocks, instead hanging around the stables. Sue, her family, and the dog gave Joan a lot of attention, which she lapped up, and I was asked to offer some healing as well.

When I met Joan it was another beautiful day; carpets of wild flowers sparkled and danced, and the air was full of chattering birds, in particular rooks calling as they attended to their nests in a nearby tree. I was glad to be outside surrounded by the hum of nature and the promise of more new life to come. Although Joan was very old, she was in good health, with lovely markings to her shaggy coat, and Sue gently stroked her before I began my healing treatment. Because I was dealing with grief, I decided to commence healing over the heart area and soon the world of healing energy and the world of bird noise blended until I could have been anywhere in any time zone. Then I was drawn to the donkey's head and knelt down by her side to be more in line with it. Joan turned to look me in the eye, transferring ancient wisdom, and it reminded me very much of the all-knowing look that my mother used to give me. Then, as I made another contact, Joan curved her neck to touch my knee, very softly with her nose before reaching forward to touch Sue's arm, the three of us linked together in spiritual vitality. I sensed that Joan knew what she needed to do and healing flowed between donkey and woman, crossing boundaries until there was only one space in one world, which they now shared.

Linking into that same collective consciousness I saw an image before me: Roxy on a beach. How very odd, I thought, usually when an equine appears before me as evidence that there is no death, just a shift in consciousness or dimension, they show themselves in a meadow or on an open plain—a natural horse habitat. Very clearly this horse was standing by the sea, and around her were cliffs and hills sloping down towards grassy banks that tumbled into the water. Roxy was happy in this environment and faced me, standing under a sunny sky dotted with a few small white clouds. I then picked up the energy resonance of Joan's thought patterns, which told me that this was where her grief lay. Being an intelligent and wise person, she was analyzing what had happened and, as with us humans when things go around and around in our heads, the loss of Roxy as a companion was bothering her. The three of us were in a healing loop, and as the donkey offered emotional release to her owner, I did the same for the donkey. There was healing enough in there for me, too, and it felt a very good place to be.

Stepping back, I mentioned to Sue what I had picked up about Roxy and studied her as an expression of wonder and bemusement crossed her features. Eventually she spoke:

> You know, I had this dream about a month ago. In it I was on an island and Roxy was with me. We walked along a beach and around us were cliffs and hills and I knew that I had to let Roxy go. I removed the head collar and rope and set her free. She tossed her head in excitement and cantered off with some native ponies, obviously very happy. Then, in my waking state I felt terrible and wanted desperately to get Roxy back but just could not find her. Of course, it was only a dream . . . and yet, you have just described that very place.

Joan had taken us to Roxy so that we could see where she lived now, and somehow Roxy had shown that same place to Sue some weeks before she had herself traveled there. It's quite incredible the healing journeys that we can take with animals—and we should never underestimate the healing power of donkeys. They can be just as potent a healer as their cousins, horses and ponies.

Later, Sue relived the dream on both the conscious and spiritual levels and saw the released horse tossing her head in the sun and the wind. Sue knew that she had let Roxy go because she needed to be free and her last image of the horse was of her cantering away. She was happy and didn't come back. It was a healing thank-you sent with a lot of love from Roxy.

Asterix and Bea

Taking on a horse that no one else wants can be traumatic, but also extremely rewarding. Bea saw the haunted look in a horse's eye and in that moment her heart connected with his and she took him home. This is Bea's story:

> Everyone told me not to take the horse on . . . but I listened to my heart and took him anyway. He had recently been badly injured,

121

having had his jaw shattered in two places due to the heavy use of a bit and a cruel bearing rein. When I first saw Asterix, he stood trembling at the back of a tiny, filthy stall barely big enough for him to turn around in; there was nothing to eat and only dirty water to drink. Large patches of sweat marked the horse's fine brown coat and every rib and vertebra stuck out. I remember whispering to him to come over so I could soothe with kind words, but the horse didn't move. There was electrified barbed wire over the door and he showed no interest in the world, head hanging low, eyes dull. The horse looked old, not the vibrant three-year-old he should have resembled. I hadn't gone to this place with any intention of buying a horse and had to be very careful what I said to be able to get Asterix away, but two weeks later he came home to me.

We spent many years steadily preparing for ridden work. First I gave Asterix a whole year of total freedom to do whatever he wanted, giving his injuries time to heal, and so that he could experience how it was to be a horse again. I worked for an equine vet at the time and he eventually gave Asterix the all clear to be ridden. Doing the reschooling, I took things slowly, for many months walking the horse in-hand on long ambles through the lanes and forests. It was great for building his trust in me and we developed a strong bond and friendship. We progressed to ridden work, although never doing much more than walking and slow trotting for a couple of years. Things were going well by then so we stepped up a gear, practicing dressage and doing some sponsored rides. For a while Asterix really shone in whatever we shared.

However, then stupidly, on recommendation of an article in a magazine, I took Asterix to see a "back man" who worked in tandem with a "dentist" (unqualified, although I didn't know this at the time). The pair of them traumatized Asterix by being extremely rough and the barbaric treatment by the "dentist" seriously damaged the jaw again, possibly even refracturing it. Unfortunately, I was inexperienced in such things at the time and did not realize what was happening or that the procedure was unnecessary and harmful.

After that, everything went from bad to worse to downright dangerous. Asterix was running into trees, so panic-stricken when ridden that I couldn't even dismount. If I attempted to make him stand still, he would rear, which I now realize was caused by excruciating mouth pain. One time I had to turn Asterix sharply into a hedge as we were on a very steep, slippery hill and he wasn't letting me get off. As we made that desperate turn, his legs went from underneath him, resulting in him rolling onto me. This, coupled with another episode when Asterix nearly placed me on top of a truck, made it quite clear that something was terribly wrong. My previously pleasant trainer then tried to bully the horse, assuming he was being naughty, so I got rid of him. Veterinary examinations followed and they were in no doubt that the horse's behavior was a physical problem, but did not know exactly what. The horse was never ridden again so that he would not suffer any more pain triggers but he still looked very unhappy.

It was at this point that I was called in to see Asterix and within minutes of laying my hands on him I had a sense of what was happening. Thumping, painful headaches were tormenting him and my own jaw started to throb and ache—a reflection of what the horse was feeling. Thankfully I was able to help through healing energy. During the process, Asterix communicated that he knew how much Bea loved him. He bore no grudges for anything that had happened, his own heart being full of unconditional love and forgiveness.

Horses are an example of utmost integrity and it is a lesson for humans to follow their example in this respect. Working with Asterix was humbling for me for, despite everything, he exuded affection, wisdom, and generosity of spirit. I didn't want to leave him that day because he made me feel so good. As we blended together, suddenly brightness illuminated the barn. I looked up, yet outside the sky was dark as rain threatened. Bea looked up, too, in wonderment as to where the light was coming from. "I thought the sun had come out," she said and I smiled. How bright the light shines from the heart of a healing horse.

Star and Annie

Life had been very hard for Annie to deal with; her childhood had been marred by an alcoholic mother, which meant that from an early age Annie had become stressed. None of her family were horsey, but Annie had sought solace at the local riding stables and when she was fourteen years old she found Star there, a small horse with a big heart. Star was the same age and after a period of time Annie was able to loan him for the rest of his life.

Two big shocks were in store for Annie a couple of years later. The first was discovering that she had a half sister, the hidden reason, she believes, for her mother's slide into alcoholism. The story that unfolded was that when her mother was sixteen years old she had become pregnant, incurring the wrath of her own parents who sent her away to have the baby. When the little girl was born, she was taken away without the mother even having a chance to hold her child in her arms. The upset and misery would reverberate throughout the rest of her life.

Then Annie's father attempted suicide, taking an overdose and driving his car into a ditch. By sheer coincidence, a passerby who was out early that morning saw the back of the car sticking out of the ditch. He decided to investigate, an action that saved Annie's father's life.

Sitting by her father's bed in the hospital Annie felt detached and unable to touch him, but when she left, she rushed over to see Star, flinging her arms around the horse's neck. She found that humans always seemed to let her down. Star never did; no matter what the turmoil of the moment, he was always there as a constant in her life, giving unconditional love.

Over the years, Annie became depressed with terrible dark spells. The confusion of her childhood and a series of failed relationships led Annie to contemplate suicide herself. Counseling, therapy, and anti-depressants followed, but what kept Annie going was that Star was always there for her. He was a soul mate, the connection between them so deep that it literally was like a bright star shining to guide her. Annie explained:

> He took me away from it all—he was my release, sanity in a world that felt unsafe. There were two extremes, the chaos of my everyday situation to being with my horse and melting into him. When we rode out together I could feel my whole body relaxing. In the middle of the heath land I would take a deep breath, let everything go and be totally at peace.

No matter how low Annie got, Star would help her. He read her moods and knew what she needed. When Annie was feeling down he would have a calmness around him that would change how she felt; it was uplifting, making her feel more positive. If Annie was upbeat, Star was his normal strutting sharp and strong self, and on those occasions when they rode out, the horse knew Annie was able to cope with him letting himself go. He loved a gallop and would shout, "Yippee, let's go really fast today," and so off they went, laughing together in their enjoyment of the day. Another benefit of having Star was that Annie could not allow her troubles to mess up her career—she needed to earn good money in order to give the horse the best of everything.

One Easter weekend when Star was thirty-two he came in from the field and started to colic, and despite Annie staying up with him through the night she had to let him go. Recounting her many years with this equine guide, Annie paid homage to her beloved partner, saying, "I wasn't overwhelmed with sadness when Star died because we had so many happy memories. I owe Star so much because he saw me through my difficult times. The hardest thing I've been left with is trying to build that sort of connection with another horse."

When I met Annie she had recently taken on a horse called Charlie who had lots of physical problems that she had not been told about when he was sold to her. She believed that ending up with Charlie was Star saying, "You know how I helped you out for all those years, and in return you looked after me? Well, I have this friend, his name is Charlie and he needs a little help, so could you return the favor and look out for him for me?"

"When I think of it like that, how could I feel bitterness—especially after all the bad times that Star got me through?" Annie reasoned. "Feeling bitter and getting down about things just takes me back to where I have been in the past, so if this is Star and Charlie working together to keep me on the right track, then that is horses healing humans . . . in motion!"

Lucy and Rebecca

Rebecca, an acquaintance of mine, told me this moving story about her experience with wild horses:

Recently I acquired some wild mustangs. They were left on the property I purchased because the owner couldn't catch them and until this happened I had never been near a wild horse before. The property is forty acres so I didn't get a very close look at them until eventually I caught them up in the barnyard and I was then able to see that they were undernourished and one of the mares was so emaciated I really didn't know how she was standing. I named her Lucy. It was several days before the horses would even try the forage that I put out for them and they finally tried what was in the buckets.

When the mustangs were first corralled, they went to the back of the area and would only come forward after I left. They jumped and snorted when I threw hay over the fence to them and would run to the far side if I stayed to watch them, so I was very cautious, always quietly explaining what I was doing. After a few weeks the mustangs were OK with me throwing the hay, standing up in front of them for short periods or walking away—and gradually I brought the feed buckets closer and closer to the fence. Soon the horses would come all the way to the fence to eat, tolerating me right in front of them, when I would talk to them, saying how beautiful they were and how sorry I was for the way they had been previously treated.

One day as I stood by the fence I noticed that Lucy had a swollen pastern. I said to her that I hoped she was not in any pain, and that it was due to an old injury—if it was recent I knew I would not be able to treat it. All of a sudden, I heard a voice say, "Thank you." At the same time, Lucy was looking at me, then she leaned forward to brush my fingers with her muzzle as they rested on the top of the fence. She softly touched my other hand before turning back to make contact with my thumb. At the time that this happened none of the mustangs had let me get too close, certainly not to touch them, so this was an incredible experience for me.

Weeks went by and the horses were doing very well so I had been thinking about turning them out to pasture. We had had some rain and the grass was coming back nicely, but suddenly Lucy stopped eating and I became very concerned about her. She followed me like she was trying to get close. Then when I had to haul water from the pond because my pipes broke, Lucy stood by me. The other horses were happily eating the hay I had put out; maybe, I thought, Lucy wants grass. So I offered her some, but after a bite she left it.

I continued to watch her and later that day saw some mucous in one nostril and what appeared to be blood on the other; this alarmed me as I know that can be a very bad sign. As I stood by the fence watching Lucy, she came into the corner to be near me and I offered her my hand to sniff, before she moved away. Speaking to the horse mind-to-mind I asked if I could offer some healing. By this time Lucy was farther away from the fence than she normally stands and I began the healing, feeling that it was needed urgently. Although I was new to this way of being and didn't really know what to do, intuitively I pointed my hand towards Lucy's chest and asked God to send his healing energy to help her. Lucy's eyes began to flicker and look sleepy and a pulse appeared on her neck that, as I watched, began to ripple up towards the head. The mare sighed a couple of times, began to lick and chew, and then dropping her head, started to eat. I was very pleased.

The next morning, Lucy had no mucous in her nose and was

back to her normal self. This was my first experience of helping a horse through a healing connection and it has been very humbling to realize the spirituality that exists in them.

All horses are receptive to our love, and you can learn whatever you need from offering a horse help.

Major and Jane

Jane had suffered bouts of depression since she was seventeen and went through many types of treatment, including hypnotherapy and psychotherapy, but the problem was never resolved. A few years later when various events were going on in her life it became difficult for Jane to share how deeply she was hurting, which led to her taking antidepressants.

Eventually, horses came into her life. First, she purchased two foals, then a riding horse called Major, who seemed to have a real willingness about him, resulting in Jane bonding with him straightaway. The horse threw Jane onto the ground one day, but the problem was traced to the saddle and as it took a while to find one to fit, Jane stopped riding.

As her depression got worse, Jane could not even leave the house except to feed the horses, before rushing back home as quickly as possible. The irrational fears that depression cause created a tremendous amount of negativity in Jane's mind and she spiraled ever deeper into hopelessness. At one point Jane even considered getting rid of the horses, but luckily her husband said, "We're not selling the horses!" because he knew how devastating that would be for her. During this period, Jane tried to handle Major on several occasions but couldn't; he would start jumping and kicking and pull away before running off.

Finally Jane's depression lifted; she came off medication and the family moved to a much nicer property. In the long term, however, things didn't go the way she had planned and another catalog of disasters struck. Jane was diagnosed with cancer, then had a bad car accident and after two such big shocks she felt very low again, so the doctor prescribed more medication, although she was not happy about taking it. Jane made a decision to spend time with the horses "just being," finding that the enjoyment of grooming triggered bouts of emotion that she felt didn't arise for any particular reason.

One day she began talking to Major then started pouring out her heart to him and, hugging the horse, told him that she loved him. When Jane had finished grooming, she opened Major's stall door to let him back out onto the pasture, but at first he wouldn't go. Jane petted him some more and after telling him she needed to groom the rest of the horses, off he went.

The next day the same thing happened: after another emotional grooming session, Major wouldn't go out when Jane opened the door. The horse stood very close by, facing her and this in itself was unusual, as he had always been rather aloof about anyone being near his head. Reaching up, Jane put a hand on either side of his face and began stroking him, but the horse did not pull away, instead looking directly and intensely at her. Jane then rested her forehead onto the horse's and stayed that way for several minutes, with tears streaming down her face. When Jane looked up she saw tears coming from Major's eyes: people say that horses do not cry, but I, too, have seen this phenomenon with horses that I have had a very close connection with.

With a flash of insight, Jane realized that she was not depressed. Major had been mirroring her emotions and wanted to heal her so that they could both be happy. She knew then that she was crying to release pent-up emotion. It was a wonderful inspirational moment and that was the day Jane quit taking the medication for good. She realized that Major had been reacting to her depression and had offered her the strength to move on. It was the most wonderful healing gift from the horse, who enriched her life through his love.

"It really is like night and day compared with how our relationship was before," Jane says. "Major showed me that horses have powerful insight into our emotions and minds, and that they are also very forgiving of our weaknesses."

Maddy and Charlotte

From an early age, Charlotte and her sister had lived and breathed horses; some nights the girls even slept in the stables with their much-loved ponies. When life was difficult or the world seemed harsh and unfriendly, the sisters would bury their heads in the patient ponies' soft necks while offloading their troubles to them. The girls' childhood revolved around being outdoors and riding, and it was a happy way of life for them both.

However, when Charlotte was eleven years old she went to an all-girls boarding school where she never really felt at ease. Living away from home meant that Charlotte lost contact with local children, and as she didn't make friends at the school she felt isolated from the community there. Being so closeted away meant that Charlotte was out of touch with the outside world, and when she entered her teenage years things started to go badly wrong for her.

One day, during some free time, Charlotte fell in with a bunch of people who proceeded to have a bad influence on her, affecting not only her manner but her studies. Eventually leaving school under a cloud, Charlotte got a job as a working pupil with a well-known rider but, becoming rebellious, she shaved off her hair and drugs took a hold. Charlotte spiraled into a dark world where drug-taking blotted out reality, affecting her physical and emotional health.

Then Maddy, a sweet-natured mare, entered Charlotte's life— although their first meeting was not auspicious. Charlotte rode the horse to see whether they clicked, and when she pointed the mare at a jump the horse unceremoniously deposited her over the fence. However, something in the horse inspired the teenager so she bought her anyway, and they went on to do a lot of things together, becoming very close.

Hard partying took Charlotte into oblivion, but through it all she could always feel the pull of Maddy's presence. The horse would call Charlotte back home, and no matter what troubles she went through, Maddy was a reason to return there, bringing the girl back down to earth. Being with Maddy was a comfortable normality. She was always happy to see Charlotte, and time spent together made the girl feel better about things. No matter what state Charlotte was in, she wanted to be with her horse, who did not judge her or offer her opinions, prompting Charlotte to recall, "She was my saint." Increasingly Maddy caused Charlotte to feel guilty about her lifestyle, because the mare would stare reproachfully into the teenager's eyes, as if to say, "What you are doing is very bad for you. Please stop it!"

In desperation, Charlotte started to seek help, and one day she had a metamorphic experience. She explained to me: "My horse was calling me, inviting me to freedom." Ditching all the people who were dragging her down, Charlotte listened to the wisdom that her horse communicated; she'd had enough of Maddy looking at her and asking, "When are you going to get yourself together?"

The horse had such a profound effect on Charlotte that, although Maddy had become part of the girl's spiritual being, Charlotte also wanted to carry a physical reminder of her. Lifting her shirt, Charlotte showed me an image of Maddy that had been tattooed on her back, depicting her as both Pegasus and a unicorn. "I have Maddy on my back forever, as a mystical being of flight and freedom," Charlotte told me. "She saved me, and I will never forget her."

Charlotte's work with horses has taken her around the world, and her love for horses has never waned. Now a mother with a young son, she leads a healthy lifestyle and runs a busy livery yard, passionate about making a difference to the lives of the horses that cross her path.

Harry and Emma

Just when I think that I have come across most scenarios, a horse opens me up to another dimension. Harry is a beautiful colored (paint) horse, mostly white with some brown markings. He stood patiently by while I worked with another horse, and when it was his turn to communicate with me, information tumbled out of him in a torrent.

First, he communicated his massive anger; he had been weaned early and the shock of having his mother suddenly gone from his life had created huge stress from which he had still not recovered. Then, at nine years old, he had been given to Emma, because the breeder that had so disrupted the horse's life could not then cope with his hatred of her. Harry also told me about this woman's alcoholism, and how she would beat him when drunk, pulling on his mouth with a harsh chifney bit until it bled and a tooth loosened. Thankfully, Emma does not drink because the smell of alcohol would bring demons back to haunt Harry.

Then an image of another mare came to me from Harry, accompanied by a profound sense of loss followed by more anger. Emma confirmed that shortly before Harry had been handed over to her, a mare that he had shared a field with for many years was taken away, compounding the horse's insecurity and resurrecting high stress levels. I then heard the horse say, "I'm worried about Emma's headaches." She looked amazed when I passed on the message, confirming that she did suffer in this way. "She's allergic to wheat and dairy," Harry continued. It was my turn to be amazed . . . never before had a horse demonstrated skills as a nutritionist or allergy specialist, but then nothing surprises me anymore about the complexity of horses. Emma was speechless, because that very week she had undergone tests for digestive problems, which had not resulted in a medical diagnosis. She was so moved at the horse's insight and concern for her that she wept on his neck. It was time for action. Could she change her life, and in doing so be an example of how horses can help us in a way that we would never have expected?

The next day Emma spent three hours in a supermarket reading labels and working out a new diet. It was an education for her in the content of foods and, despite finding everything rather overwhelming to start with, Emma persevered with cutting out wheat and dairy and started to see the effects immediately. Her headaches went, as did the stomach cramps and bloating. One day at a conference she was given a meal cooked in butter, despite her asking for non-dairy food, and had a severe attack of pain, making her even more determined to keep to the new regime. Emma gave up smoking, too, and overall her energy levels soared and her mood improved.

The relationship with Harry blossomed, with him becoming much calmer. Emma sensed that Harry now trusted her and she, in turn, became confident in her abilities. Having taken steps to sort out her health and well-being, Emma learned that she was in control of her life. When you know that a partner really understands you, it makes you feel special and therefore you become closer to them for that honor. It becomes a reciprocal process and Emma's last report to me ended with: "Harry is such a wonderful horse, with so much to give and I feel lucky to have him in my life—I just hope I continue to do right by him." I know she will because woman and horse now have a positive connection, one with the other.

10 What's in a name?

There are times for all of us when we feel anxious, or have lost our way. Being with horses can transform darkness to light so that constraints lift, a way appears before us and we have a sense of belonging. It's a miracle how this can happen.

It is now proven that horses are strategic and exceptional partners in facilitating increased awareness and insight of body language and the senses, as well as developing confidence, trust, and assertiveness. Talk therapies alone will not always fully resolve trauma—one of the advantages that horses have over human therapists is that we can freely touch them and they can touch us. Touch is acknowledged to be healing in itself, when both giving and receiving. Also because horses do not use verbal language, in listening to them we shift from focusing on words and their interpretation, to allowing inner wisdom to speak directly to us.

For these reasons, the role played by horses in many varied areas is becoming increasingly recognized, as it can be uniquely constructive, stimulating learning, insights and progressions that don't transpire any other way. It is possible to become students of the horse in various disciplines, including coaching and self-development, education, riding therapy, psychotherapy, and experiential learning. When these modalities are offered by people with true equine empathy, recognizing the horse's special attributes as well as having proven people skills and sound training in both fields, the arising experiences can be extremely rewarding.

To maximize the potential of emerging changes, equine-facilitated programs should ideally have a multidisciplinary approach. Trained human facilitators can help support and provide insight into the spiritual landscape that unfolds within someone through their proximity with horses. Unlike working with human therapists, whereby people can come to view them as a crutch, horses have an uncanny ability to activate a self-guiding process whereby we learn to stand on our own two feet. As Amy Blossom, Executive Director and founder of Reins of

133

Change, an organization dedicated to providing mental health services, points out: "It is our job as professionals to get out of the way and let the horses do the work."

An overview of types of horse/human healing

The following section offers a brief overview of the main areas in which horses partner humans to help people.

Centers of education with riding therapy

These centers offer educational and personal development through being with horses. For those motivated by equines, the horse becomes the heart of new understanding, learning, and teaching. Being in an equine environment can redress imbalance in people's lives as horses give biofeedback about inner processes, which may be just what is needed for a dynamic shift in behavior to take place. Taking part in naturally occurring routines and activities with horses helps us with literacy, numeracy, and social skills. People quickly learn that if they do not look after a horse's every need, it will not survive, recognizing a parallel in their own lives and the value of self-care. Young people who attend courses in which horses are included for teaching purposes automatically seem to allow themselves to be transported to learning via this interaction, and their exploration of skills is facilitated.

Horses teach about teaching

As we go through life, different things unfold and the horse stores up lessons for us. Anyone can be touched when the horse is at the center of learning, not only the children and young people interfacing with the horse, but their teachers too will be influenced by the four-legged tutors. Buffy Lacey, an educational specialist for children with learning difficulties in Scotland, has discovered new aspects to teaching through using horses to help youngsters gain confidence and an interest in life. In conventional teaching, a day is planned and children directed to follow guidelines. Horses make that sort of approach impossible, because if you want to learn from them you have to let them be themselves, allowing the lessons to evolve accordingly. Buffy explains:

Both horse and child are vulnerable. If the teacher goes on a power trip, then they will both pay lip service, but you never find out who the true core being is. It's too easy to *want* the horse or child to do what you ask, but being dictatorial means you crush the spirit of a young person, just as you will with a horse. Horses have taught me to look at the small details, to not rush ahead and to wait for the young person to make a move, just as the horse needs time to respond. And to be as patient as the horse is with us.

While visiting a horse therapy center I heard about a fifteen-year-old girl who was an elective mute. At school the girl made little social contact and selected isolation from her peers, but as soon as she was given a horse to interact with, her whole demeanor changed, to the extent that the normal teaching staff reported never having seen her smile so much. As the girl touched, stroked, and groomed she talked to the horse, describing what she was doing and telling him he felt soft. As the days went by she initiated conversations with others regarding the horses, yet taking the lead in an exchange of ideas was something that she had never done before. Some of the sessions with the horses involved working in pairs, and for a girl who shunned company it was assumed that this was going to prove very difficult, yet she took to it, even becoming the leader in her pair. When I heard that the girl talked about loving the horse it made perfect sense; there had been outpouring of love on both sides. The girl could give of herself without anything being expected or demanded of her, in response to the unconditional love from the horse, giving just because he could.

Therapeutic riding

There are places that offer riding as a therapy but without the educational and special needs classroom work. Therapeutic, or adaptive, riding involves an individually designed program based on the physical, emotional, and mental needs of the person (child or adult), including any social/learning/communication disabilities and limitations. The staff involved have been trained to accommodate these aspects and goals will vary as the individual progresses. Through the act of riding, physical strength, mobility, coordination, and balance improve. Concentration and verbal skills are integral in learning to ride successfully, as are social skills such as interaction with the horse, making human friends, and respecting authority. Benefits reported include improvement in confidence and self-esteem as well as life skills.

Riding for the disabled

This area includes riding as an activity for people of any age with a disability, in either a recreational or a competitive way, and under the guidance of qualified instructors. Riding for the disabled groups are dedicated to improving the lives of people with disabilities, enabling them to improve health and well-being, delivering a lasting therapy that not only benefits mobility but encourages confidence and self-worth while having fun.

Hippotherapy

" Horses are an indicator of human behavioral and emotional states. "

This is a term given to physiotherapy that utilizes the natural movements of a horse to help people regain physical coordination and mobility. The pelvic movements of a horse at walk, through the corresponding movement of the human pelvis, enable a rider to learn or relearn skills and movements that may have been compromised or lost. This can also include speech, respiration, and body awareness.

Equine-assisted psychotherapy

This is a particular combination of psychotherapy and horses not normally involving riding; the idea being that certain issues may rise to the surface for an individual as that person handles or interacts with various horses. These can then be dealt with by the psychotherapist and may include anger, fear, anxiety, low self-esteem, relationship problems, motivation issues, and lack of confidence. It is the horses who raise issues by mirroring and reflecting what is happening inside the person, which is revealed through energetic movement as well as the person's body language. As the horses sense what is going on, they accordingly act upon it.

There are many organizations and individuals worldwide involved with this type of work and one pioneering exponent is Dr. Allan Hamilton of Rancho Bosque in Arizona, a Harvard-trained neurosurgeon and professor of surgery. His association with horses began as a hobby but he soon recognized their therapeutic potential.

As well as for adult cancer patients, sessions for children suffering from cancer bring amazing results, helping them to cope better with their illness. "Cancer is a big powerful thing," explains Dr. Hamilton, "but through the horses, the children can learn skills to help them be in control rather than out of control. Horses become a metaphor for learning to deal with feelings of being overwhelmed by something far bigger than yourself, as well as a true catalyst for healing and empowerment." Importantly, too, contact with horses is vastly different from medical treatment programs and can help improve the relationship between parents and children because having fun together through these incredible animals brings another dimension to their relationship.

Horses helping doctors

Another area where Dr. Hamilton has pioneered equine-assisted therapy is in helping doctors hone their bedside manner skills as physicians. He states:

> Whenever doctors are interacting with a patient, doing uncomfortable invasive things or having to impart bad news, we really need to have the patient's trust. This is exactly the point of the work with horses, because the handlers need to use gentle, nonverbal cues to persuade the horse what to do. The horse gains trust and becomes a willing partner. This is exactly what we need patients to do—to join us in the healing effort rather than being afraid of what we are doing to them. With patients, like with the horses, it is up to the doctor to figure out what works best with each.

Jennifer, a first-year medical student, says the course has made her more aware and sensitive of her small movements, such as when she walks into a room to interview a patient. Although Karl, a third-year student, found working with the horses hard, it helped him become more tuned into nonverbal communication. Such is Dr. Hamilton's success with the doctor-horse program that it has now been adopted in six medical schools across the U.S.

There are, of course, those who criticize the scheme, saying that these classes with horses are too touchy-feely, at the expense of the vital medical science that students must learn. From my own point of view, however, I would much rather be seen by a doctor who respected me as a unique sentient being rather than one who treated me like an anonymous object. We need more empathic approaches in this world, not less, and it's wonderful that the role of horses is increasingly recognized as helping a wide variety of people to understand themselves and each other.

Equine-facilitated coaching

In this field, people experience self-development through interaction with horses by understanding how they are metaphors for human behavior. Businesses now also use this type of coaching to help employees develop leadership and communication skills and to enhance workplace relationships. Horses, of course, are the master guides and catalysts for these sorts of discoveries as they teach about energy, helping people learn how to choose and generate energy that they want to take back to other aspects of their life.

As Andrew McFarlane, founder of Leadchange—a high profile U.K. business coaching company—explains:

> Today's business executives operate in a knowledge economy. Companies employ people more for their minds and hearts than for their ability to perform physical tasks. Management by control and command no longer works. Leaders need to challenge, inspire, and enable. They have to communicate vision and "walk the talk." Horses help people develop practical leadership skills that translate to the workplace; they facilitate this process by offering immediate and honest feedback.

Having spent some time with Andrew and with Liz Morrison, I witnessed successes taking place. One man, a team leader, whose problem was that he had a "low energy" group of people working for him, realized that his team members—like the horse he was working with—were reflecting his own low energy state. As he raised his energy, the previously lethargic horse perked up and trotted for him. Through this he discovered how to increase the team's energy by managing his own. Another project leader who was visualizing the failure of a particular project could not get the horse to walk with her. As soon as she changed the images in her mind and visualized a successful outcome, the horse followed wherever she went. One of the most dramatic revelations came for a chief executive. The horse he initially worked with took no notice of his commands, but as soon as he assessed his own feelings of enjoyment, the horse responded and was soon following him. This made the man aware of a better way to lead his company; he wanted his employees to enjoy their work and through the horse realized he could not force people to have fun.

"Before introducing them to the horses," says Andrew, "I like to ask delegates, 'If I wanted to do your job and be brilliant at it, what personal qualities would I need?' The answers always describe qualities we need in order to effectively interact with horses. Horses don't do role-play, and so what we learn from them is directly transferable to all areas of life."

Equine-guided education

Ariana Strozzi, author of *Horse Sense for the Leader Within*, who has set up the Equine Guided Education Association in California, has been bringing the magic of horse wisdom to people since 1990. Her work encourages growth and learning through the "eyes of the horse" and offers a supportive experiential learning environment in which the horse becomes the guide for human development, growth, and learning. A combination of human educators and equine guides offers incomparable reflections geared towards developing self-knowledge and self-responsibility.

Through the process of evaluating the individual's pattern of behavior, perceptions, and performance, the student/client is encouraged towards a healthy self-image and exploration of new practices for achieving personal and/or professional goals. The human educator understands how to allow the horse to reflect each person's strategies in such a way that he or she can receive this often intense feedback in a safe and supportive process. Ariana and her horses reconnect people to land and nature, so that they can rediscover what has heart and meaning for them, forgive what has been broken, find hope in times of uncertainty, and walk a path of integrity and grace. Being in harmony with nature revives the spirit, releases pent-up emotions, and guides people towards the right action in balance with the greater good.

> "Excellent communicators, horses respond to how people feel in an unbiased way and, completely tuned into human emotional states, reflect them back."

Equine-facilitated experiential learning

Founded in 1997 by author, journalist, and trainer Linda Kohanov, Epona Equestrian Services is a unique experience. Named after the ancient horse goddess Epona, a symbol of healing, the center based in Arizona, is a collective of trainers, riding instructors, educators, counselors, psychotherapists, and artists exploring the power of the horse/human connection and it has received international acclaim for its exploration of inner healing. People from around the world have gained a greater sense of physical, mental, emotional, and spiritual balance by taking part in the programs and workshops. Through a holistic approach to the equestrian arts, clients explore topics such as assertiveness, stress reduction, emotional fitness skills, strengthening self-esteem, and personal empowerment. People find that they are helped to reawaken long-forgotten abilities that are capable of healing the imbalances of life.

A creative spiritual experience with the horses is offered, including music, art, writing, dance, exercising intuition, and even evening events drawing on moonlight inspiration. That's a great idea, because why should we only spend time with a horse during daylight hours? Theirs is a twenty-four-hour world and horses have much to teach us at any time.

The Epona center makes much of honoring the horse and the fact that their equine residents, living naturally as a herd, form the basis of learning and healing. Together and individually the herd members inspire, challenge, nurture, and enlighten the workshop participants, who interact with them for a few days or weeks, as well as the staff members, who work with them and care for them daily. Horses, too, benefit from taking part in the Epona work in that it provides a healing space for them. Having had personal experience of a couple of Epona sessions, with instructors Ruth Le Cocq and Anna Pell, I can vouch for the gentle yet empowering nature of the work, which treats both horse and human with utmost integrity.

Bringing out the best

Evidence of the human-healing effect of horses is increasing as more people realize what incredible catalysts horses are for this to take place. The following are just a couple of examples.

David and Louise at the Fortune Centre of Riding Therapy

The renowned Fortune Centre of Riding Therapy at Avon Tyrell, U.K., offers three-year residential courses where young people with special needs can learn through interaction with horses. It was there that I met Louise and David, two young people for whom traditional methods of teaching and learning had failed to help or make an impact on them. Eighteen-year-old Louise was coming to the end of her three years and David, aged twenty, was in his second year at the center. Like many of the people there, Louise's schooling had been troubled and she had become disruptive in class before dropping out. She hadn't liked school, she told me, and hated sitting at a desk because she was more of an outdoor person. As she had ridden since she was six years old, her potential with horses was identified and a place was found for her at the center. At first, however, she didn't like it at all and went through a phase of feeling very unsettled.

"Then I started seeing the light and what I could achieve; the horses help you in this," she told me. "I didn't want to spend my whole life lazing around, I wanted to make something of my life, and through the horses I am doing that."

Louise's literacy skills had been very poor when she started at the Fortune Centre and she went on to explain how looking after the horses had made her want to read, because she was motivated by them. There was so much to do during the day; things that the horses couldn't do for themselves and she liked attending to their needs. When she is sad or needs time to herself, Louise always goes to talk to the horses: "I like my time with the horses—just to be with them. It gives me peace and quiet." Having turned her life around so successfully, Louise's ambition now is to travel the world through work with horses.

Like Louise, David had been around horses since he was very young. His childhood had been happy but he found learning at school frustrating because, even though he knew the answers to questions that teachers asked, he found it difficult to express himself. This led to David being bullied and his reading suffered badly as a result. David's mother heard of the Fortune Centre and got him a place there, which has been the making of him. At first, David was overwhelmed by the fact that he was surrounded by friendly people—he had come from a school where he had no friends and was feeling depressed.

"When I came here, my heart lightened," he said, "and I have never regretted one minute of my time here. Everyone is friendly because we all have a common interest, and since being here I get on better with people."

David warmed to his topic and began to astound me with his insight and understanding. Profoundly, he added that when we understand horses we are then more able to understand people, and that the key part of interacting with both was emotional sensitivity. He further explained that there was a direct relationship between horse and human emotional responses, for example, being tense or relaxed influences the relationship. David mentioned that he had a sixth sense around horses—he could sense pain and unhappiness, not just through body language but also in his heart and mind: "I have always felt this way about horses but have never been able to put it into words until I came here."

Two horses in particular, Bradley and Aslan, had a special meaning for David. People were scared of Bradley due to his large size, but the horse was himself nervous of people. David explained what he had learned from them: "Bradley has taught me another aspect of size, that being big can be more scary than being small." As he was a tall boy himself, I thought perhaps that was a reflection of how David used to feel before his experiences at the Fortune Centre helped him to become more confident.

Aslan, a young, sweet-natured but highly sensitive horse, had taught David to respect space and to be aware of his moods. "Through the horses you learn to work as a team and to respect others around you . . . but most importantly to respect yourself," David observed. "If you don't respect yourself, then you don't live properly. Self-respect gives you trust in yourself and your abilities. Before I came here I didn't think I had any options for my future but the most lowly work; now my ambition is to go on and train in cabinetmaking and restoration."

When I asked David to sum up what was so special about horses, he gave me the following amazing statement: "The most special thing is the bond between the horses and the people . . . it becomes one living thing. Horses can sense your emotions and if you are upset, will come to comfort you. They are like big, walking, furry mothers."

What a fabulous description of the healing horse!

The Suffolk Punch Trust

Talking to Bruce Smith of the Suffolk Punch Trust, I heard how troubled men had been helped by horses. Inmates of Hollesley Bay Prison in Suffolk have been doing community work with horses on the site since 1938 (the trust, a charity, took over in 2006). They not only do manual work but take horses to shows and help with schooling. The men, many of whom have violent pasts towards other people and who rarely have previous experience of being around horses, seem to become protective of them, greatly enjoying time at the farm.

Inmate Jim went there in the coldest part of one winter and helped to turn the horses out into the paddocks. Full of joy at being out of their stables, the horses would gallop around as Jim followed their every move, saying, "I never get tired of this, just watching them." A couple of years later, Bruce came across Jim at a horse show. Jim explained that he was there with his new work, telling Bruce, "It's true, there's no money in horses, but I'm really enjoying it and they have kept me out of trouble." Jim's past had led to the breakdown of his marriage, but the horses had brought him back into contact with his wife and children as they now got together to ride. The pleasure this connection brought them was something that none of them could have foreseen.

Another success story concerned Ken, a man who had served a long sentence, and who Bruce would frequently find softly talking to the horses. One day he explained to Bruce that arriving at the prison he quickly learned that it was deemed a sign of weakness to show any sensitivity; "but with the horses it's different," he said, "because they are non-judgmental. They don't accuse me of being weak. I give them affection and they offer it back."

Many other inmates have gone on to remain involved with horses, including one who became a farrier (he never tired of telling people that cleaning a huge pile of harnesses was his first introduction to horses), and another who has joined an equine healthcare group. No one has ever absconded from working with the horses, which must be a measure of how much the men enjoy their time there. "There aren't many people I'll say goodbye to when I leave here," Derek, another inmate, said, "but I will miss the horses and want to come back to visit them."

Ex-racehorses are now also involved at venues where other inmates go for community service placement. Most of these horses have had a troubled past, many having been weaned too early, roughly handled, and their needs neglected. Therefore, the men can identify with them as jointly being in rehabilitation. This helps them to develop an increased sense of self-awareness through contact with the horses; an empathy unfolds. As Derek succinctly put it: "These are beautiful animals and it is a joy to be with them and share their breath. We look after them and they look after us."

A wonderful gift of horses is that they have no preconceived opinions about people, allowing those from troubled backgrounds to present a side that, for some reason, has been hidden away. It takes a lot for a "tough" person to admit to emotional sensitivity, yet the diplomacy of horses often results in this taking place.

> **"**The horse needs us to realign so that as a team, transformation can begin.**"**

The healing horse needs helping

Despite their strength and speed, horses are emotionally open and forgiving. Their openness is one of their attractions and an aspect of their nature that makes them so special to us. This leads to the inclusion of horses in all kinds of situations. They are vulnerable through their innocence and openness, and when involved with horses in any form, whether riding, handling, treating or with interaction/therapy

143

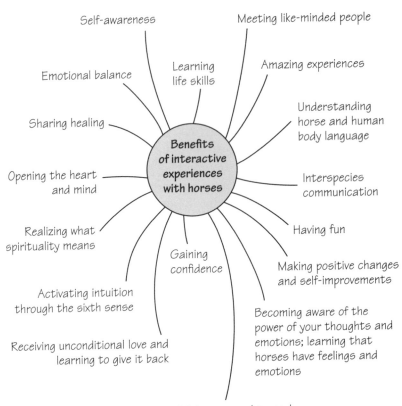

Self-awareness

Meeting like-minded people

Emotional balance

Learning
life skills

Amazing experiences

Sharing healing

Understanding
horse and human
body language

**Benefits
of interactive
experiences
with horses**

Opening the heart
and mind

Interspecies
communication

Realizing what
spirituality means

Having fun

Gaining
confidence

Making positive changes
and self-improvements

Activating intuition
through the sixth sense

Becoming aware of the
power of your thoughts and
emotions; learning that
horses have feelings and
emotions

Receiving unconditional love and
learning to give it back

Connecting with horses soul to soul

work, it's paramount to be aware of their vulnerability. Horses are teachers, guides, educators, facilitators, therapists, co-counselors, partners, and the key to whatever transpires in their presence. They are the foundation of experiential activity and catalysts for change, including the spiritual, and so deserving of full recognition. They never lose sight of the work that they need to do with us, even when they themselves are overlooked. A human failing found in all equine disciplines is to become biased towards people needs (including those of the self) and to lose sight of horse needs. Equilibrium is a vital quality to hold, otherwise the lessons of the horse are not actually understood; it's like stepping into a school class halfway through a term and not being able to fully get to grips with the subject.

Some organizations give information about the horses as well as the human facilitators, including the names, backgrounds, and particular gifts the horses may possess—although many make only a passing reference. It appears that generally the emotional, mental, or physical welfare of the horse is not always considered a priority, yet often there are pages of a code of conduct pertaining to humans. In my view, it's tantamount to saying: "This horse interaction stuff works, but they are only animals after all and we humans are far superior." A key concept in any work with animals is that it should be viewed as holistic . . . seeing a horse as an equal can open our eyes to the vision that all life has equality.

While a great deal of research has been done to show the benefits of human interaction with animals during therapy, very little has been undertaken from the animals' standpoint. Yet horses have to perform under a variety of conditions, both ridden and non-ridden. Unpredictable human activity, including sudden movements, raised voices, and a fluctuation of moods, can place stress on a horse. Not addressing the vital physical, mental, and emotional health of a horse, but nevertheless using him or her in therapy work, ridden work, or workshops, is like sitting by the bedside of a sick person and saying, "I have this problem that I was hoping you could help me with."

Welfare of the riding therapy horse

There does not appear to be a formal physical welfare system in place for horses used as therapists. In riding therapy for people with physical disabilities, as part of the team, certified physical therapists play a significant role in using the horse to help improve balance, mobility, and movement of the rider. Organizations may list their physical therapy staff members but I have never seen an equine physical therapist mentioned on any literature. Although I do know of places that have physical therapy checks on horses when a problem is noticed, it is vital for a more structured approach, examining horses regularly before something obviously manifests (and that may be a long time after the horse first felt uncomfortable, by which time much damage may have been done).

Respecting the horse means making sure that he or she is pain-free, remembering that a horse influences rider movements—the reason for their use in riding therapy work. I have watched classes where horses with stiffness or otherwise uneven movements caused the rider to flop and twist to one side, thus potentially aggravating both of their problems. Also, carrying a rider who is not able to balance or control movement naturally due to their own physical disabilities, will have an adverse effect on the horse's back, and can either create problems, or make existing ones worse.

Horses are often donated to riding therapy centers, perhaps after a hard career in other disciplines, or after becoming unsuitable for their work due to injury—although many such horses should be honored with retirement. People think that therapy work is easy for the horse, but it is not, for the reasons outlined above. Using physically compromised horses to carry physically compromised riders has integrity only if both have the same level of attention paid to their needs; at present, it is far from this ideal state of affairs. I would like to see it become mandatory that all riding therapy organizations have qualified equine physical therapists on the staff team, who as a matter of course check each horse regularly to identify any problems and advise on their suitability for the riding program.

World-renowned veterinary physical therapist Amanda Sutton, for ten years a committee member of the British Association of Chartered Physiotherapists in Animal Therapy (ACPAT), and who has also been an equine Olympic team physical therapist, says: "Any abnormal gait or dysfunction in the horse will have a ripple effect for the human sitting on that horse's back. Certified physical therapists first qualify with people before qualifying to work with horses; therefore, they are uniquely placed to understand the horse/rider influence, and can advise/treat accordingly."

Horses bring enormous pleasure to people whose lives are blighted in some way and words cannot describe how much this priceless gift means in enhancing lives. However, it must be a two-way pleasure and not be at the expense of a horse's well-being. A happy, pain-free horse reflects healing energy to all those who sit on his or her back. Overlooking a horse's problems does not benefit anyone in the long term.

The horse is not a tool

Horses are sentient beings, meaning they have thoughts and feelings. I find it disrespectful to read about or hear a horse described with terms such as a "therapeutic vehicle" or a "tool." The horse is no more a tool than you or me—in fact, a tool is an inanimate object that I keep in my garden shed or garage. Using such terms is far off the mark regarding not only understanding horses but the relationship that people should have with them. Acknowledgment must be given to the horse's unique and special role, by placing them alongside human therapists, not beneath them.

146

Choosing a workshop

It's tempting for anyone with access to horses to set up in equine- facilitated work as a way of making a living or continuing their own emotional exploration. Working on another's problems does sometimes attract people who see it as a part, even unconsciously, of their own development. Because horses do not differentiate between the energy states of facilitators and clients in their vicinity, it is vitally important that facilitators make sure that they are not taking their own unresolved issues to workshops and, equally, that they know how to process for themselves any emotions and triggers that may occur during a session. All of us are continually processing the influences on our lives from birth onward and a practitioner of any discipline needs to have become aware and settled before working with members of the public. Issues cannot be blocked out but must have been dealt with. As a safeguard, facilitators must be properly trained and qualified in disciplines such as psychology, psychotherapy or counseling, as well as having taken training with the leading centers that teach how to incorporate horses into the fields of learning, coaching, and education.

For those interested in attending a workshop, talk to several facilitators before deciding, and discuss your views on horses as spiritual beings as well as finding out about the qualifications and length of training of those involved. If the person talks overly in jargon, perhaps he or she is showing signs of introversion in the topic, bearing in mind that the lessons of horses are dynamic and unique to you. Most learning situations arise from people having their own individual experiences.

Some facilitators lack sensitivity or have a controlling nature. Their way of working is to be challenging, making clients feel uncomfortable, or they may encourage conflict, thinking that is a way to stimulate change. The horse in the setup will feel all arising conflict energy from whichever direction it comes, influencing his or her responses. Fundamental in any personal work is that the human facilitator should establish boundaries of what he or she may or may not do with both horses and humans. Shaming either (and it happens in all equine fields, unfortunately) is never acceptable nor constructive behavior. Facilitators should be highly skilled in working at a deep level and have empathy and awareness of their responsibility to all beings. Gut feeling is your inner voice talking and can act as a guide to making a choice. This also helps improve confidence for making any decisions in life.

> "To acquire knowledge, one must study, but to acquire wisdom, one must observe."
> *M. Vos Savant*

Essential requirements to honor and protect horses as facilitators

It should not be assumed that a horse will enjoy or be suitable for the type of work considered, or with all situations/people, just because the horse is available. Assessment needs to encompass a wide variety of behavioral, physical, historical, lifestyle, and age parameters.

Horses must be given a choice—to work or not—and be able to choose how they will interact with the human. Horses must have enough space to make a choice of interacting or not.

The very fact that horses are worked with because they read energies means that they will be affected by them and in individual ways. A check should be made before and during every session to see whether he or she should be used as a facilitator or riding horse that day.

If a horse shows signs of undue stress, or discomfort, the session should be ended.

In work with highly emotional or disturbed people, horses should not take part for more than a short period per day, and not every day.

Horses should have a "human buddy" to monitor them in the same way that human therapists have a mentor that they link to. After each session, horses should be checked to see if they are relaxed or showing signs of stress.

Honest feedback will only come from horses that live a natural herd lifestyle, rather than using suppressed horses going through the motions. This will lead to false interpretation if a horse shuns human company or allows anyone to do anything with it, irrespective of what the horse actually thinks about the people in the session.

Being turned out into a herd after a session helps horses to recover from any stresses that their lifestyle raises. Horses should not spend a lot of time in a stable or stall and should not be isolated from other horses.

Horses should have days off every week and regular holidays just like their human partners.

Physical checks should be made daily for pain/discomfort and regular gentle hands-on bodywork given as a routine, as well as vet, dentist, and farrier checks.

Mentally or emotionally disturbed horses or distressed, anxious, or unsettled horses and those in pain should not be worked with.

 A variety of work should be considered where applicable so that horses do not become bored or frustrated.

 Human facilitators should have expertise in reading a horse and in all work the needs of the horse must be considered—after all, the business revolves around the horse.

 Last but not least, after the culmination of every session, the horse should be thanked by all the people who have shared time with him or her for everything that has been offered and taught. This applies to whether the interaction was ridden, handling, or at liberty. We need appreciation and so do horses because it creates uplifting energy that is good for the soul.

We must repay horses for the blessing of being able to share time together by taking care of them.

11 The horse's viewpoint

Where knowledge comes from does not need to be pondered over as far as a horse is concerned. When we shift our own perspectives, then we start to get an inkling of this. It's an intense, expansive, and magnificent revelation.

To allow horses to teach, help, and heal, we must always look at the world from their perspective. This aspect of awareness, of becoming horse-like, will help us to become not only more fulfilled, but more complete as human beings. To do this and see the world from the horse's viewpoint, we need to monitor our own expectations, judgments, and prejudices.

A viewpoint is how we consider something to be, and there are many aspects and facets to this, depending on our approach. Horses do not restrict themselves with a set opinion of what may be going on, but use senses—including the sixth sense—to see the whole picture. Perceiving things as if for the first time and using the same range of senses will help us identify a horse's way.

People have often expressed to me that once they started looking at things from the horse's perspective—and there can be no dichotomy from the spiritual aspect—they felt a huge sense of relief, like a weight lifting from their shoulders. On a few occasions while meditating with horses I have had what is described as a transcendental experience, whereby I became transported to a level beyond the everyday. I cannot begin to describe it because the sum total is condensed to an instant vision, and in that flash I have thought, "Ah, so that's what it's all about." As my rational mind stepped in to be analytical, the insight was gone again but, bizarrely, it seemed that by transcending the level of being, all knowledge can be condensed to fit onto a pinhead. It is always a vividly blissful cognitive experience, as though I am summoned to awaken from a conundrum. These occasions have made me want to be a being of completeness like the horse, to be constantly in synch with who I am, as well as every other creature on the earth . . . and beyond. I can only imagine how complete horses feel when left to their own devices and why it is so agonizing for them to exist by non-empathic man-made rules without freedom to live according to the laws of nature.

When a horse enters our life, we become attached to a guide that has no concept of our material existence. Whatever the horse's viewpoint of us, it is not based on where we live, our work, or social life; the trappings of a human lifestyle do not have any relevance, although other things are meaningful. When warmth soothes a horse's back, he knows the sun is shining, and when wetness spatters his face, that the rain has come. When a bird lands by his foot, a rabbit runs past, or the wind stirs, it is all part of the moment; the horse observes everything and misses nothing in his view of the day. A horse knows what is enduring and what is passing, both physically and spiritually, accepting the difference. When we expand how we view the world and share information, endless possibilities for learning and growth present themselves; when we look only in one direction, then much can be missed. Frequently, other people can also trigger a thought process that leads us to finding out something new and relevant.

Our commitment

If we want the best from someone, and all horses are "someone," we need to be a good role model. In everything we do, we must ask ourselves, "What is in this for the horse?" Development, awareness, motivation, learning, connection, and healing all take place on many levels simultaneously, in the seen and unseen realms, which is why it's important to consider everything from the horse's perspective as well as our own. Horses are amazing creatures and they deserve nothing less

The whole picture

Physical reality can be used as a basis for establishing our viewpoints, but this narrow field of perception will limit our vision and may prevent us from seeing the whole picture. When we consider something through our spirituality, utilizing the overview of universal energy, we can adopt a wider perspective.

The art is to see the detail simultaneously with the whole picture. When only detail is considered, it's like taking hold of a handful of sand; the grains fall through our fingers as we lose sight of the beach.

Horses look at things both ways because they are aware of physical presence in tandem with the non-physical sphere of energy as it links continuously both to themselves and to us. It's a skill worth emulating.

than our commitment at all times to take care of their every need, including the spiritual. The horse and the human are both part of the same equation and if the human does not do his or her bit in reviewing attitudes, behaviors, and ways of thinking, then the horse's lessons will be missed. Taking something from the horse to give to the human is not constructive. If at the expense of a horse the human gains, then the process has failed because it lacks value and is empty.

Through their connection to the free spirit in us, horses transport us beyond our limitations into the boundless, where they see and know everything. We all have this potential, but it's frequently horses who remind us of how to open up and become fully aware. The more that the human race evolves, the more it seems that it needs reminding of the essential truth of relationships with non-human forms of life. Horses are exemplary in opening our eyes, ears, hearts, minds, and souls to just how much we need to connect to other beings.

Increasingly, as learning from animals is becoming a vitally important stage of human evolution, people are coming forward to make peace with horses, nature, and themselves. It's a wonderful revolution as kindred spirits support each other's endeavors. The concept of the healing human and the healing horse is not considered odd anymore; it's the new normal and the horse responds with faith when we do the best we possibly can, generously wanting us to succeed.

Conversation with a horse

I dreamt I had a conversation with a horse.

Before me I could see horses of all ages and colors. I yearned to be in their midst, to run and play with them and, most of all, to find my place in their society. I took a few faltering steps to join the herd, then some big strides forward. The clouds parted and rays of sunlight illuminated my path. A pale horse came to greet me, a vision of wondrous beauty.

"You wish to speak with me?" the horse asked.

"It would be an honor if you have the time," I said quietly.

"I have your lifetime to answer whatever you need to know," the horse replied.

"What is the most important thing I should learn?"

"You can learn that being anxious about the future means you forget the present and so live in neither. The present is what we have together and is full of meaning. Take care of it, see the life around you and become its caretaker.

"Learn that we look at the same things, yet see differently; appreciate another being's perspective and intelligence, for it holds truth.

"Learn not to compare yourself with others, and treasure your uniqueness. It is your essence that we reach out to help.

"The most important lesson is to become the embodiment of unconditional love, which we show by example," the horse concluded.

I thanked the horse for the advice and, humbled, said: "As a race we are not always good to you and my heart is heavy for that."

The horse replied, "Knowing that you care is enough; we forgive mistakes because that is part of learning."

Blending with the horse, I felt myself become the earth, the sky, the seas, the stars, and all that there is.

"Your dream is our dream," said the horse, "to create a peaceful world. I am always here whenever you need me to guide you."

12 Hands and hooves in partnership

Colleagues and acquaintances from around the world share these lessons from being around horses.

I have been lucky to work with many horses over the years, but one particular relationship I have had stands out. I first came into real contact with the horse when caring for him after a problem at an event, and was struck by his patience and the trust that he placed in me that night, even though he didn't know me that well. After this I started looking after him full-time and over the years we have developed a very special relationship.

The horse has led a long and sometimes hard life and has limited trust in humans, always presuming that something bad is going to happen, so when a horse like this finally puts his trust in you, it becomes very special. His personality is very quiet but through the connection that we have he tells me small but heart-touching things, like when he is thirsty or excited, or perhaps that a day is not a good one and he would rather stay in the field. I have been out hacking and looking at the cloud-filled sky, thought that we must hurry before rain arrives . . . and without an aid, this amazing horse has popped into a trot to get us home before the first raindrops.

When we go out together, be it at a competition or just out for a ride, it is an outing as friends. My horse puts his trust in me and I can honestly say that it has been a privilege to be allowed to enter his some-times fragile world. This makes us more aware of the responsibility we have towards animals, especially when we are using them for our own pleasure. This horse has opened my eyes and heart increasingly to their feelings and fears, and taught me so much in many ways—sometimes I feel quite humble when he offers me his trust and friendship. I hope that more people will spend the time in this busy world listening to their charges. They would receive their efforts reflected back to them tenfold.

Jackie Potts

Jackie is a full-time international event groom based in England, and was awarded the title Groom of the Year 2006 for her exemplary work with horses.

At first I wasn't able to put into words the happy feelings and the loving bond I have with horses that heals them as well as me. I had gotten stuck in the veterinary point-of-view taken over by pain, because here in Spain I work with a lot of rescued animals and see many badly treated ones; I could only describe anger, sadness, and frustration towards these situations. I realized that first I had to heal my emotions before I was really able to heal the horses on a soul level. Still I was not able to describe what my deepest feelings for these marvelous creatures are. The brain can be so much stronger than the heart. So I took myself back to the time my brain didn't control my heart; the time I first made a connection with a horse.

When I was eleven years old, a pony called Turbo arrived in the pony club. It was love at first sight for both of us. As a child, you don't talk about unconditional love, but in your heart you feel it. I was always talking to Turbo, in our own secret language, and I shared with her all my secrets, my sorrows, my questions about life and she gave me information, answers you do not expect to come into the mind of a young girl. Now I think that horses can be our spiritual guides, or they can be a strong link between us and our spiritual connection to the universe. I am truly convinced that horses understand our deepest wishes and I believe that if you wish for something from your heart, your horse can make dreams come true. That's the sacred gift from them to us.

Horses are the best meditation and relaxation teachers; when I come home to them from a hectic day, the stress is gone immediately. I don't know whether horses consciously remove the stress and give back good energy or whether I become relaxed because they almost oblige me in their gentle way to become centered when around them. I certainly feel my body relaxing when I ride bareback. It's like the stress is drained away through my spine down the horse's back and legs to the ground, then comes back up the same way, completely clear and full of liveliness. Even looking at horses in a field can give my soul healing and the relaxing sound of grazing is like an endless prayer to my ears. There are a million reasons why I love horses and connect with them. The most important one is that horses stimulate my six senses in a very strong and profound way, touching my soul deeply.

Emmanuelle Vandendriessche DVM, cert. Vet Chiropractic, cert. Trad Acupuncture
Emmanuelle was certified as a veterinary surgeon in her native Belgium and now
practices in Malaga, Spain
www. animalwellnessclinic.net

I think of the many different approaches or modalities to equine-assisted experiences like a young tree growing and branching out in all directions.

While one branch of horse sense for the human potential tree is reaching in the direction of equine-assisted psychotherapy, there is another limb reaching into the educational system in the form of equine-assisted learning. There is yet another branch reaching into the metaphysical world and others are budding into areas such as corporate team building, working within the prison systems, working with troubled teens and disenfranchised street youth and another in a direction specific to battered and abused women. As much as I am thrilled to watch the equine-assisted tree branch out into so many learning, growing, and healing directions, I try to stay focused on what I consider to be the deep reaching roots of the tree—how horse sense can help each of us as individuals to learn how to "tame the dark horse that lives within our shadow nature."

Far more than mere metaphor, the practical work with horses that people might refer to as training techniques are, in fact, essential life skills that we can all use to not only train the most challenging of competitively natured horses but also to better train ourselves to live happier, healthier, more balanced lives. After all, qualities that a horse looks for in its leader, such as consistency, self-assurance that is sensitive and non-threatening, awareness balanced with focus, receptivity balanced with decisiveness and boundaries, and caution balanced with courage, are all very real lessons that a horse desperately needs to see in its leader in order to truly feel comfortable and confident about knowing that he or she is in good hands, and exactly what we want and need to see in ourselves.

With horses, they don't always or often give us what our ego wants—but they do always give us what our soul needs. Where so many people seem to get stuck in life is when they are faced with needing to answer the difficult, or often paradoxical question, as to whether or not a situation or an issue they are involved in requires that they find the serenity to accept what they cannot change or whether or not they are experiencing an issue where they must have the courage to change what they can. It has been my experiences with horses, and the lessons I have learned from horse sense, that shows me how to lay the inner lion down with the inner lamb, so that I can find the balance in my experiences that leads to "the wisdom to know the difference."

Chris Irwin

Chris is a much-read columnist and the author of Horses Don't Lie *and* Dancing with Your Dark Horse. *Based in Alberta, Canada, Chris coaches throughout North America and Europe in groundwork, riding and driving and, with his wife and training partner, Kathryn Kincannon-Irwin, directs the retraining of veteran thoroughbred racehorses at the Makers Mark Secretariat Center at the Kentucky Horse Park in Lexington, where his pioneering work in both horsemanship and equine-assisted personal development (EAPD) is endorsed by the Thoroughbred Retirement Foundation.*

Loving horses since I was a child, there was no doubt ever in my mind that I was growing up to study and "be" with horses. I could "hear" what horses were thinking and feeling, which made riding and training horses easy, but having people friends more difficult. I wondered why all people could not understand horses, because they communicated so clearly. As a wildlife behavioral ecologist studying wild horses throughout the West, the more time I spent with various wild groups of horses, the more I realized that horse culture was all about social friendship, not dominance. Sure there were dominant horses, like there are dominant people, but sustainable, functional horse herds were built on strong social bonds of the leaders. Where there were not strong social bonds, often there was no leadership and the herd became unstable. Horses, like most social mammals, learn most of their behaviors, but without a good functional horse herd not many horses learn how to "be" horses. The same can be said for humans. We all exist in the same whole system of life and the more we learn about our connections to nature, to ourselves, and to all the life around us, the more whole we feel. Horses are a connection to consciousness.

My journey into horse culture has been a journey into awareness. Horses have taught me how to "be" and slow down my brain waves to communicate clearly. They have taught me the importance of unconditional friendship and loyalty. Horses have guided me to value emotional intelligence more than mental intelligence and have helped me learn how to match vibrational energy with all creatures. Understanding the importance of spatial awareness and respect, horses have coached me how to help people set clear boundaries and understand "safe space." What started out as a scientific pursuit to understand horses has been a journey into consciousness and the meaning of life. My life with horses, and people, continues to be truly an enchanted kinship.

Mary Ann Simonds, BS, MA

*Mary Ann has a BS in wildlife biology and range management and a Master's degree in interdisciplinary consciousness studies with a focus on human-animal interactions and healing. She also has graduate specialization in organizational development and leadership. She teaches and coaches internationally with the Equestrian Science Institute. Mary Ann is based in Vancouver, Washington.
www.maryannsimonds.com*

The message that I receive from horses on a daily basis is that they want to be understood. Horses are no longer the beasts of burden of the past but unique spiritual beings that are misunderstood by many of their owners. Horses try with body language to communicate their wants and needs, their fears and pain, but more often than not people dismiss a reaction as a vice or say, "but my horse always does that." Horses want, and need, their pain to be acknowledged as real and I will often see a change in a horse even before any therapy has begun, so relieved is he or she that someone is listening at last. Horses receiving treatment for the first time will often turn and look at me with wide eyes, amazed that someone is finally addressing their problems.

Often I hear people berate their horse, expecting him or her to go out and win them ribbons. If only people would understand that horses feel the meaning behind words; horses need to be shown love and respect so they can work as a team. So many horses dream of being "just a horse," hating their lifestyle and restrictions. It is a pleasure to work with clients who are in tune with horses and satisfying to see that they are becoming increasingly numerous. I notice that more and more people, too, are turning away from competing and are having a horse in their lives for pleasure or even to have as a friend without riding, to experience their teaching and gifts. I am truly blessed and honored to be making my living working with these beautiful beings and to be able to make a positive difference to the lives of those that I come into contact with. Horses are soul mates here to support our spiritual growth and for us to learn more about ourselves. This is their connection to us.

Shirley Calder
Shirley is an equine dentist and the instructor for the European School of Equine Bowen Therapy in New Zealand. She is also a New Zealand Equestrian Federation coach.
www.shirleycalderequine.com

During the time that I have been working professionally with horses, they have taught me key factors about life. In order to understand horses and succeed in whatever I undertake with them, I have to be willing to listen to them and, when necessary, to make changes in myself. Horses point out my strengths and weaknesses, so that I constantly strive to improve my way of being. I am very grateful to horses for this learning opportunity. I now feel that the art of riding and training successfully is not only about teaching horses, but also about adapting myself in such a way that I respond to their needs. Only by doing this can I achieve harmony and true success. This, in turn, leads to the ultimate prize—a deep connection with horses.

Christina Wiederkehr-White, BHSII Registered Instructor
Christina is a Swiss event rider now living near Swindon, England, where she has a schooling and training facility. She is also a selected trainee to the Eventing Coaching Team of Great Britain.
www.wiederkehreventing.com

159

After spending several years working in the U.K. as a veterinary physical therapist, I returned to my country of birth, South Africa. Working within the animal treatment industry here in a third world country takes on a whole new meaning. Poverty and hardship are so much a part of everyday life for more than forty percent of the population that many of our animals are neglected and, sadly, abused. I felt the calling to get involved with a cause that could benefit our animals but also uplift the impoverished children of South Africa, and crossed paths with the SAID Foundation, a humble little charity based in Cape Town. Their aim is to encourage a better interaction between animals and humans in a process through which children are assisted in developing compassion and respect for the value of all living creatures, together with an understanding of the interconnectedness of life. It provides the knowledge and understanding necessary for children growing up in harsh conditions to take responsibility for the choices they make, and behave according to humane and ethical principles. Their projects emphasize practicing and reinforcing kindness, care, and empathy through nonformal education processes. There are so many horses in dire need of rescue, but for every one horse rescued and re-homed, another three take its place.

Through another intended project, rescued horses will be homed and rehabilitated to have a whole new chance and function in life. Children from the informal settlements ("shanty towns") near Cape Town will have the opportunity to attend special days and weekends at an equine rehabilitation center. The aim is to heal both horse and child through their interaction and connection with each other. I have felt the healing and calming influence that horses have and, given the chance, the children will have the opportunity to spend time with these remarkable animals. Through the gifts of horses, these children could, in turn, grow up to be adults that will have respect for all animals and, hopefully, the circle of abuse will be broken.

Christelle van Wyk
BSc. Physiotherapy, PG Dip. Veterinary Physiotherapy
Christelle runs a private veterinary physiotherapy practice in Cape Town,
South Africa, and is a trustee of the SAID Foundation.
www.thesaidfoundation.co.za

Brothers Om and Jai share a struggle for survival with Raju, the mule who earns a living for their family in India. Several years ago, the brothers' father died and left behind a sick wife, seven children, and the mule. At the time, Om and Jai were around seven and five years old and their mother had no option other than to send her sons to work, and their only hope was Raju. They started working in a brick kiln and Raju worked as a family member, cooperating in their need as a true and faithful friend. The Brooke mobile veterinary team and community animal health workers were working in the area and four years ago Dr. Shabir, the vet in charge, came into contact with the brothers and their mule. He noticed these two boys as very polite and sensitive owners, always keen to know about the Brooke's treatments and welfare messages. According to Dr. Shabir, "Raju is around fifteen years old now and his condition is good—he is fit for work. I wonder how these small boys keep their animal in good health in such adverse circumstances." Om and Jai always bring Raju for vaccination and deworming in proper time and regularly clean Raju's saddle to protect him from wounds and skin infections. Both brothers are so caring about their animal that they immediately take Raju to the Brooke team whenever any problem arises. Jai said, "How could we neglect Raju? He is our only hope in the absence of our father. He gives us support to live and he feeds us. Without his help, we could not find a way out from our crisis period."

Dr. Shabir reports, "I am thankful to these young innocent children that I have never needed to attend any emergency for Raju because they give priority to prevention of problems. I wish every owner thought along the same lines. It would save equines from suffering and, in turn, they can help people to survive."

Nilanjana Chowdhury
Nilanjana is a spokeswoman for the India branch of the Brooke.
The Brooke is a charity operating across nine countries in Asia, Africa, Central America, and the Middle East. The aim is to help working horses, donkeys, and mules in the world's poorest communities, through free veterinary treatment and community animal welfare education programs. The Brooke has over 750 highly skilled staff working directly in the field.
www.thebrooke.org

In a nutshell, what I have learned from horses is that they make decisions based on how they *feel*, not on what they *think*. Like wild animals, horses rely on their intuition, precognitive and sensate feelings when relating to humans, other animals, and their surroundings. When a horseperson can open their mind to this concept a whole new way with horses becomes possible. How different our lives could be if we learned to stop thinking so much about how we are doing and how others regard us and trust that we already know what is going on. Horses listen and respond to what is happening on the inside of a person, sensing when someone is afraid, timid, angry, calm, balanced. They want to know if we really care about what we are asking of them, if we are inspired by the possibility of oneness. Their ability to sense who we are behind our tools *is* their primary source of communication. The various tools and techniques that exist in the horse world are secondary and tertiary forms of communication that often rely on conditioning the horse into a specific type of performance though subordination.

Imagine the horsewoman who comes out to the barn after a hard day's work. She's still uptight from the stress of her day; her face is pinched, breath short, jaw clenched. Her horse fidgets and tosses his head and she grooms the horse faster, still not breathing. He fidgets more. After saddling her restless horse, she enters the arena only to have him wiggle and prance around while she tries to mount. Still the woman doesn't notice that the horse is just mirroring her mood. She tightens her jaw more. "Damn horse," she whispers. He flares his nostrils. "I'm just reflecting how you are feeling," he whispers. In her frustration she wants to scream, but then remembers *her horse's attitude has everything to do with her attitude*. She stops what she is doing, takes several deep breaths, empties her mind by feeling her feet on the ground and the breeze on her face. After several minutes she feels centered and mounts the horse now standing quietly beside her. She didn't need any tools or fancy techniques to quiet her horse; she just needed to quiet herself, focus on how she was feeling, not on what she was thinking. She reconnected to her desire to meet the horse as a partner, not a dominator. Basically, she had allowed herself to become a student of the horse. This shifting of perspective, from dominator to partner, allows a new world to open up.

Ariana Strozzi

Ariana began her horsemanship career at the age of seven, winning many championships in English and Western riding disciplines. Based in California, she is the founder of Intuitive Horsemanship™ and Equine Guided Education, and author of Horse Sense for the Leader Within. *www.strozziranch.com*

Eighteen years ago, when Jack entered my life, I had no idea of the impact he would make. I was angry, lacking in self-confidence and with low self-esteem. I didn't have a great childhood, without good role models to help develop my social skills. I had also failed to follow my heart in so many areas of my life.

Jack was not an easy horse. The level of frustration I felt when training him was intense. We could not communicate what it was that we wanted from each other, and there were many "experts" telling me what I should do. One instructor got on him to "sort him out" and I watched helplessly as, yelling, she spun him around in circles. His eye caught mine and I felt his fear and pain, but I didn't have the courage to stand up for him. Afterwards, as I hugged Jack's sweaty neck I vowed that I would never let anyone bully either of us again, and I haven't.

My actions alienated peers, friends, and family, but I had to set some acceptable boundaries in my life. It was hard, I was lonely and I wasn't liked, but I saw the relationship with Jack blossom. It was all I had to hang on to, but his strength and loyalty saw me through. Jack has been my greatest role model for integrity and authenticity. He is solid and dependable with a sense of humor but no pushover. When I went through a few years of depression, Jack was always there, stoic, quiet but always challenging me to raise the bar. He has taught me to listen to my heart, to develop true awareness, and to be passionate about whatever I do. He has helped me to become a better leader of people and horses, and to never accept anything less than the truth.

Jan Barley
Horsewoman, therapist, and coach, Jan lives in Gloucestershire, England.

Horses taught me to love again, and this time without fear. My work has opened me up to how trusting any horse can be when layers of abuse are peeled away. They continually present themselves to work with us and, if lucky, they find a human being willing to learn from them. I have so much respect for how horses assess us and our humanity, that I began to use them to check out any prospective love interest. Angus, a Cleveland bay police horse, and Red, an ex-racehorse, would give me very honest nonjudgmental opinions that helped me become more discerning regarding my choices. Sometimes it would be a simple offer to accept a pat, or a subtle tilt of the head to move away from someone's energy. They were always discreet. The more that I accepted the horse's assessments and found that they matched my own instincts, the more I was able to have faith in my own inner guidance. I now follow their connection example with my new partner, resulting in becoming aware of the subtle tones of his voice, the way that he carries himself in different moods, and sensing when he needs something from me. I can respond without judgment as Angus and Red have taught me, accepting what is required to maintain a harmonious environment where we enhance each other's lives. The horse friends in my life have taught me how to give and receive the best, and with ease.

Catherine Bird
Catherine is the author of A Healthy Horse the Natural Way
and lives in Sydney, Australia.
www.happyhorses.com.au

We can discuss aspects of this fascinating topic but we will never cover it all. I am a person who is so passionate about these wonderful, generous creatures that I want to pass on all the amazing things I have learned from them, before and since I set them free into naturally living herds around twelve years ago. In my head I could do it concisely and coherently in a matter of hours, with my horses on hand to demonstrate relevant points. Of course, I couldn't even scratch the surface, but still I try! The main point that I have learned is that with horses there are no rules and no formula. The minute you think, "Horses do this/are like that," one comes along that says, "Ah, but, except when . . . !" We have to learn to be totally open, utterly without ego, and completely unconditional in our love for them. Then, and only then, will they show us their true abilities, which go far deeper than we often appreciate. In our world today, there is so much that we can learn from the horses, not least of all a sensitivity to nature on our planet and a connection to the underused intuitive side of our brain. It is neverending, but I relish the thought of going out and learning still more today.

Lucinda McAlpine

Lucinda is based in Devon, U.K. She is a dressage rider and trainer,
expert in natural horse management, and developer of the intuitive riding approach.
www.lucindamcalpine.com

People tend to think of racehorses as highly strung nutcases. Of course, they are no such thing. Any behavioral vices they may have come from the misunderstanding of them, leading to their mistreatment. People visit us here and comment that we are really making a difference, providing idyllic surroundings, special care, etc. Yet when I look into the eyes of the horses here, they look back with some gratitude maybe, but also with a deep resonance of balance. If I'm overexcited about a win or a new treatment we think we've discovered, Saucy Night will look at me and say, "That's good, you're learning." And then with a twinkle he'll add, "Took you a while," and my egotistic rush will be grounded and I'll realize that, of course, he's right.

Another day I'll walk into a paddock with numerous worries buzzing around me and Dream will walk up and give me a big shove as if to say, "Hey, don't bring that stuff down here while we're eating." Of course, you can only laugh and in that moment you are back in balance. Many great sages talk about being present and "in the now" and we buy books and go to conferences to try to achieve this, and yet it is easy to see that all horses are always perfectly present naturally. Racehorses also teach us about spirit and that it is the most precious gift we have. Once a horse has lost his spirit, it is terribly difficult to rekindle. They teach us that in our children burns a desire to be, and to be magnificent, and that careless action can cause irreparable damage. In their magnificence, racehorses show us the sheer joy of running, that competition can generate greatness, and that even though our Formula One cars are fast, they cannot match a horse in flight for grace, beauty, and pure expression. Horses teach us every day.

Eamonn Wilmott
Eamonn is Managing Director of Horses First Racing, Sutton Veny, England.
The racehorses at this facility live naturally in herds on organic pastures, and are
barefoot where possible. An extensive team of natural therapists and holistic vets help
the horses to be in optimum physical, mental, and emotional health.
www.horsesfirstracing.com

Conclusion

Whenever I am with a horse, I reflect on what I am being offered. I have learned that instead of wondering what I need to know, I only need to want to learn and revelations will begin. Every time I am in the company of a horse, he or she has the potential to join me on an extraordinary spiritual, emotional, and mental journey.

The more I have opened myself up to this way of being, the more I have found that I can achieve in terms of increased understanding. Heightened levels of awareness present themselves in many ways. Among the numerous things that horses open my eyes to is that they are incredible, highly evolved beings of great wisdom. One of our tests as humans is whether we listen to horses and their truths. When we do, it helps us evolve so that we begin to move forward with whatever we are undertaking. The horse is a gateway to a revolution without war or hurt, encouraging us to be at peace with ourselves and, therefore, with each other.

Somewhere out there is the horse, or horses, that can help each one of us to find whatever our soul is seeking. Horses need us to share a healing journey with them as much as we need to undertake it. It's a wonderful life-enhancing experience. Through their amazing healing lessons, horses can fill our lives with magic, our hearts and minds with love, and our days with color.

Useful information

Margrit Coates
P.O. Box 1826
Salisbury
Wiltshire, England SP5 2BH
Website: www.thehorsehealer.com
Information on books, relaxing music CDs for pets and horses, DVD, workshops, and consultations.

Margrit's CDs and DVD can also be obtained worldwide from www.newworld music.com.

The Fortune Centre of Riding Therapy
Avon Tyrrel
Bransgore
Christchurch
Dorset, U.K. BH23 8EE
Website: www.fortunecentre.org
People with special needs learning through horses. Information on residential placements. The Fortune Centre also offers courses, training, and qualifications in equine assisted therapy.

Dr. Deborah Goodwin
Website: www.psychology.soton.ac.uk/?uid-dg1
Ethologist and lecturer at Southampton University, U.K. Her website includes articles and papers about horse behavior, management, and welfare, based on sound scientific research.

Human-Equine Alliances for Learning (HEAL)
Website: www.humanequinealliance.org
HEAL founder and therapist Leigh Shambo, MSW, has developed a curriculum for building relationships with the horse that is powerfully transformative. The HEAL approach provides the perfect context for effective therapy and personal/ spiritual growth; it is equally valuable for equestrians who seek a richer, more conscious relationship with their horse. HEAL also offers training programs for professional counselors and riding instructors.

Epona
Telephone: 520-455-5908
Website: www.taoofequus.com
The home of Epona Equestrian Services, founded by Linda Kohanov, is Apache Springs Ranch, Sonoita, Arizona. Extensive horse facilities include board, care, training, and riding lessons. There is also a conference center, visitor accommodation, and a retreat center. Website has information on equine facilitated experiential learning workshops, apprenticeships, and professional training. Also lists international Epona qualified instructors.

Mary Ann Simonds
Telephone: 360-573-1958
Email: enchantedkinship@yahoo.com
Website: www.mystichorse.com
Mary Ann is an equine behavioral ecologist, coach, horse—human relationship specialist, and trainer with regular clinics and events worldwide. Her website offers resources including books, CDs, DVDs, and videos.

Rancho Bosque
Telephone: 520-760-4468
Email: info@ranchobosque.com

Website: www.ranchobosque.com
An equine center of excellence in Tucson, Arizona, founded by Dr. Allan Hamilton. The center holds numerous seminars and clinics in equine assisted therapy.

Ariana Strozzi
(Equine Guided Education and Intuitive Horsemanship™)
Telephone: 707-876-1908
Email: ariana@strozziranch.com
Website: strozziranch.com,
www.leadershipandhorses.com
Ariana is a pioneer of equine guided education and offers one-on-one sessions, seminars, workshops, clinics, and professional training courses. Resources available on the website. Ariana's facility, Strozzi Ranch, is based in Valley Ford, California.

Chris Irwin
Website: www.chrisirwin.com
Training and seminars for horse and rider, also in equine assisted therapy, by international rider and author Chris Irwin. Resources available on the website.

Australian Equine Behaviour Centre (AEBC)
Website: www.aebc.com.au
The Australian Equine Behaviour Centre has been conceived and developed by Dr. Andrew McLean, together with his wife Manuela. Andrew holds a PhD in horse training psychology and is the author of several books. The AEBC center offers training systems relevant to horse and rider.

Rutgers Cook College
Website: www.esc.rutgers.edu
The website of Rutgers Cook College, New Jersey, contains useful information for horse caretakers.

Equine Studies Institute
Website: www. equinestudies.org
Dr. Deb Bennett is one of the world's leading experts on equine anatomy, conformation, and biomechanics. Also a skillful teacher of riding, training theory, and technique. Numerous courses and training opportunities on the website.

Reins of Change
Telephone: 847-464-5177
Email: amy@reinsofchange.com
Website: www.reinsofchange.com
Amy Blossom is the Executive Director/ Founder of Reins of Change, based in Illinois, offering equine assisted psychotherapy.

Eagala
Website: www.eagala.org
Eagala (equine assisted growth and learning associated) is a worldwide non-profit organization developed to address the need for resources, education, and professionalism in the field of equine assisted psychotherapy.

Advice Websites
Website: www.horsewomen.ning.com
Useful networking and advice website.

Website: www.naturalhorsetalk.com
Online radio show and numerous interviews and articles by international horse experts.

Website: www.naturalhorsepeople.com
Website with resident experts offering helpful advice.

Resources to help horses

Books

The Injury Free Horse
Amanda Sutton MSc Vet Physio,
MCSP, SRP, Grad Dip Phys, ACPAT
Cat A
ISBN 0 7153 110 X

The Treatment of Horses by Homeopathy
George MacCleod MRCVS, DVSM,
Vet FF Hom
Revised and updated by Nick
Thompson BSc (Hons) Path Sci,
BVM&S, Vet MF Hom, MRCVS
ISBN 1 8441 3295 1

The Veterinary Care of the Horse
Sue Devereux BA BVSc MRCV
ISBN 0 85 131 924 6

The International Veterinary Acupuncture Society (IVAS)

2625 Redwing Road, Suite 160
Fort Collins, CO 80526
Telephone: 970-266-0666
Website: www.ivas.org

American Holistic Veterinary Medical Association

Telephone: 410-569-0795
Email: office@ahvma.org
Website: www.ahvma.org
Maintains a directory of members for re-ferral purposes.

American Physical Therapy Association, Animal Rehabilitation Special Interest Group, Orthopedic Section

APTA, Inc.
2920 East Avenue South, Suite 200
LaCrosse, WI 54601
Telephone: 800-444-3982
Website: www.orthopt.org

The Brooke

Website: www.thebrooke.org
Donations, subscriptions, legacies, and fundraisers always much needed to help working equines, in the world's poorest communities, lead a comfortable life.

Special thanks

There are numerous people and horses for me to thank. Inspiration can come from something that someone says, even one word can lead me to take out my notebook and start scribbling. Thank you, therefore, to everyone that has crossed my path—clients, friends, and colleagues. Special thanks go to Sue Devereux, a very busy acupuncture vet and author, who read sections of my manuscript and made very helpful suggestions. Veterinary physical therapist Amanda Sutton continues to inspire me with her passion to help horses and her phenomenal knowledge.

I am grateful to Dr. Deborah Goodwin who has advised me on horse behavior and ethology. I am also delighted that this book has put me back in touch with ecologist Mary Ann Simonds, and I am indebted for her input regarding equine behavior, psychology, training, and handling.

I am indebted to my family for the support that they have given me. My husband Peter for his moral support, my stepdaughter Emma for cheerful phone calls, and my sister Sue for the good vibes.

The photos in the book are from several sources, some taken by myself, and others by Jon Banfield, Barry Witcher, Andrew Kempe, Wendy Chisholm, and Jane Cook, to whom I am very grateful. The horses who so generously modelled for the photographs are Cleaver, Wexford, Walter, Gigolo, Tetua, Barney, Abervail Dream, Zorro, Digby, Johnny, Playboy, Jasmine, Joyce, Merlot, Shizaz, Amber, and the New Forest ponies. The amazing photograph on the cover is by internationally renowned photographer Sabine Stuewer. I think that her image of an Andalusian horse in a poppy field perfectly illustrates equine spirituality, wisdom, and freedom.

Equine artist Jenny Arthy has kindly donated the drawings on pages 8 and 16 and on the chapter headings, and her amazing work can be seen at www.jennyarthy.com. The illustrations on pages 86 and 153 are by Rodney Paull. The cartoon on page 153 is taken from an original by holistic horsecare consultant Kenny Williams, husband of Lisa Ross-Williams, the host of the "If Your Horse Could Talk" radio show (www.naturalhorsetalk.com). Thank you everyone for your creative input.

I am, of course, extremely honored that Linda Kohanov, someone whose writing and work I greatly admire, has written the foreword for this book. I am indebted to Linda for taking the time out of her very busy schedule to do this. It is wonderful how our love of horses has connected us in this way and brought our worlds in touch, one with the other.

Finally, thank you to the horses and ponies who have guided and inspired me during the process of writing this book. Without you I would not have been able to write a single word.

Photography

Jon Banfield: pages 14, 66, 90 and 176
Wendy Chisholm: page 27
Margrit Coates: pages 30, 40, 50, 89, 98, 114, and 131
Peter Coates: back cover
Jane Cook: page 76
Andrew Kempe: page 166
Sabine Stuewer: front cover and page 165
Barry Witcher: pages 109 and 150

Index

173

Other Books from Ulysses Press

ANIMAL REIKI: USING ENERGY TO HEAL THE ANIMALS IN YOUR LIFE
Elizabeth Fulton & Kathleen Prasad, $14.95

Ideal for animal lovers who are interested in exploring complementary therapies, this book provides a thorough introduction to Reiki, including step-by-step instructions for treating animals.

NATURAL REMEDIES DOGS AND CATS WISH YOU KNEW: A HOLISTIC CARE GUIDE
Dr. Viv Harris, $14.95

A hands-on, remedy-based care guide that allows pet owners to naturally improve their pets' health day to day and holistically treat many common ailments.

SECRETS OF THE PEOPLE WHISPERER: A HORSE WHISPERER'S TECHNIQUES FOR ENHANCING COMMUNICATION AND BUILDING RELATIONSHIPS
Perry Wood, $12.95

The author shows how the techniques used to develop trust and understanding with a horse can work equally well with humans in personal, business, family, and romantic relationships.

TALES FROM THE DOG LISTENER: 28 SECRETS TO BEING YOUR DOG'S BEST FRIEND
Jan Fennell, $14.95

In *Tales from the Dog Listener*, world-famous dog trainer Jan Fennell goes beyond basic techniques to the illuminating real-world stories of dogs and people learning to live together with mutual love and respect.

To order these books call 800-377-2542 or 510-601-8301, fax 510-601-8307, e-mail ulysses@ulyssespress.com, or write to Ulysses Press, P.O. Box 3440, Berkeley, CA 94703. All retail orders are shipped free of charge. California residents must include sales tax. Allow two to three weeks for delivery.

About the Author

Margrit Coates is a world authority on healing for horses and a renowned equine communicator. She gives consultations, runs workshops and lectures internationally, including visiting the U.S. Margrit lectures to postgraduate students of Animal Behavior at the University of Southampton, U.K. She is the cofounder of Holistic Pets, a clinic offering natural treatments for horses and pets.

In addition to writing columns and articles for magazines and newspapers, Margrit makes frequent appearances on both television and radio. She has produced music CDs and a DVD to aid the healing of horses and pets. She is the author of the groundbreaking books *Healing for Horses, Horses Talking,* and *Hands-on Healing for Pets.*

Margrit lives in the New Forest National Park of southern England where she loves to walk among the wild ponies. For further information, please visit www.thehorsehealer.com.